Pottery cat and dog; buff clay, fired and painted in dark
brown and reddish brown; the stylized animation of these
little animals is typical of work made at Ameyaltepec. Oaxaca.
Height 4″ (10.2 cm.) *From the collection of Jean and Russell Ames.*

Other books by Florence H. Pettit
with photographs by Robert M. Pettit

BLOCK PRINTING ON FABRICS

AMERICA'S PRINTED AND PAINTED FABRICS

AMERICA'S INDIGO BLUES

and two books for young people:

HOW TO MAKE WHIRLIGIGS AND WHIMMY DIDDLES

CHRISTMAS ALL AROUND THE HOUSE

MEXICAN FOLK TOYS

FESTIVAL DECORATIONS

AND RITUAL OBJECTS

by Florence H. and Robert M. Pettit

with 57 full color and 317 black and white photographs,
14 graphics and drawings

HASTINGS HOUSE PUBLISHERS
New York 10016

LIBRARY OF CONGRESS CATALOGING IN PUBLICATION DATA

Main entry under title:
Pettit, Florence Harvey
Mexican Folk Toys

  Bibliography: P. 183
  Includes index.
  1. Toys—Mexico. 2. Festivals—Mexico.
3. Indians of Mexico—Games. 4. Indians of
Mexico—Rites and ceremonies.
I. Pettit, Robert M., joint author. II. Title.
GN560.M6P47   394′.3′0972   78-15864

ISBN 0-8038-4709-2

Published simultaneously in Canada by
Saunders of Toronto, Ltd., Don Mills, Ontario

Printed in the United States of America
Designed by Al Lichtenberg

CONTENTS

ACKNOWLEDGMENTS   8

INTRODUCTION   11

I THE TOYS OF MEXICO   13

Toys in Mexican History
Colonial Mexico
The Twentieth Century
Mexico Today
The Mexican Family
Games Children Play
Modernization; Summary

II MINIATURES   57

III RITES AND RITUAL OBJECTS   65

Myths and Witchcraft

Bark Paper; Otomís of San Pablito
Huichols of Jalisco, Nayarit and Zacateca
The Coras
The Seris

Masks of the State of Oaxaca 77

IV THE TOYMAKER AND ARTISAN AT WORK 79

**A Brief Encyclopedia of Mexican
Materials, Methods and Magic**

Abalone Shell	Feathers	Papier Maché
Amate Bark Paper	Fibers	Rabbit Fur
Aniline Colors	Flowers	Reed
Beads	Glitter	Spanish Moss
Boar Bristles	Gourds	Straw
Broomstraw	Glass	Tempera Paints
Chia Seeds	Lacquer	Tin
Chickpeas	Lead	Vanilla Beans
Chicle	Leather	Wax
Clay	Masks	Wire Springs
Copper	Nutshells	Wood
Corn Shucks	Palm Leaves	Summary
Cotton	Paper	

**V A CALENDAR OF TRADITIONAL
MEXICAN FESTIVALS AND FIESTAS** 111

The Year's Events

JANUARY 113

FEBRUARY 115

MARCH 116

LATE MARCH—EARLY APRIL 116

APRIL 123

MAY 124

JUNE 125

JULY 126

AUGUST 127

SEPTEMBER 127

OCTOBER 127

NOVEMBER 128

DECEMBER 137

Fireworks 145

**VI MARKET DAYS, WHERE THINGS ARE MADE,
MUSEUMS AND SHOPS** 167

    a. Market Days—Tianguis—through the week
    in Mexico 167

    b. Where Toys, Handcrafts, Decorations and Sweets
    are Made 170

    c. State and government-sponsored Popular Arts
    Museums and Shops in Mexico; Stores in Mexico
    and the United States 175

VII GLOSSARY 173

    a. Spanish-English 177

    b. English-Spanish 180

VIII BIBLIOGRAPHY 183

NOTES ON THE PHOTOGRAPHY 184

CREDITS 185

INDEX 187

ACKNOWLEDGMENTS

The authors give their sincere thanks to these
people who were especially helpful, in one way
or another, in the preparation of this book:

Jean and Russell Ames, Oaxaca
Bob and Betty Raab, Oaxaca
José Moreno Innes, Oaxaca
Yvonne Forbath, Guadalajara, Jalisco
Irmgard Mezey, New Canaan, Connecticut
Eleanor D. Bronson, Stamford, Connecticut
Constance T. Young, New Canaan, Connecticut
Jorge Cueto, La Jolla, California

and quite a few gracious and hospitable
artisans of Mexico

To the Memory of Josephine and Jessie

Pottery *Tree of Life* with Adam and Eve in the Garden of
Eden; painted with tempera colors, with flowers, birds, etc.
made separately and attached by wires. This is a 20th
century Mexican decoration, made in many sizes, some as
large as 40″ tall (1 metre), and the trees are a customary
wedding present. Some are candelabras, and the motifs are
changed for Easter and Christmas seasons. Height about 30″
(76.2 cm.)

INTRODUCTION

Lion, mold-pressed papier maché, painted with tempera colors pink, black and white. 5″ × 3½″ (12.7 × 8.9 cm.)

What is a toy? The word is learned at an early age in any of dozens of languages by young people around the world. They have all heard the phrase, "Pick up your toys." A toy is described by the Encyclopedia Britannica as "a trinket, a bauble; something for a child to play with; something diminutive; something that can be toyed with. A child's plaything."

Webster's dictionary says, ". . . something that is merely amusing or diverting; a thing to play with, specif. an article, often an imitation of a living or manufactured thing on a small scale, designed and made for the amusement of a child, or for him to use in play."

The definitions tell us what toys are, but they cannot tell us what toys mean. Nothing is said about the magic, fanciful importance of toys in a young person's life. No reason is given for the deep, abiding love felt by grown-ups for certain toys which through the years never let go of their imagination. It is not easy to explain why playthings keep hold of the affections of people of all ages who find in them a sort of talisman that represents a second, small cosmos that is unfailingly bright and joyous. To think of a toy as "merely amusing or diverting" is to be blind to the importance and wonder of playthings. A toy can be a child's best friend, and is sometimes his only friend in the big and complicated world around him.

Perhaps Charles Eames, the North American designer, also has a point when he says in his film, *An Eames Celebration:* ". . . toys are not really for children, they're for grown-ups, especially for grandparents."

There is a fascination about the marvelous little objects that stimulate the imagination of youngsters and are a lasting delight to adults who have hung on to their powers of make-believe. The playthings of Mexico have a distinctive aura of folk fantasy about them, but when they deal with real things grown small, the interpretation is charming and lively.

The word *decoration* gets even shorter shrift than *toy* in the reference books. Webster says it is an *ornament*; Roget's Thesaurus says: "adornment, embellishment, elaboration, garnishment and frippery." When one sees a small Mexican town decorated for a fiesta with hundreds of colored paper banners, strings of bright lanterns, palm leaf arches and paper flowers there is an unmistakable feeling of excitement and happy anticipation. The visitor asks, "What's going on here?" The effect is much more than mere garnishment.

It is necessary, then, to see the traditional hand-made toys and decorations of Mexico to know what they really are, and in order to understand that they are much more meaningful than mere amusements or frippery. Mexican toys are gay and funny, and fiesta decorations really do raise the spirits. Who can resist such a cheerful combination?

Some of the most decorative crafts in Mexico are the ritual objects used by a certain few Indian tribes. Their colorful designs have deeply meaningful connotations in mystical tribal ceremonies and are as handsome as they are mysterious.

Will traditional Mexican Indian crafts survive modern advances in the country, and can the individuality of Mexico withstand the dilution that often comes with the so-called progressive advances of technology? Octavio Paz, Mexican poet and philosopher has faith in the constancy of the crafts of his country. He says: [In Mexico] "craftwork is not even national; it is local. Indifferent to boundaries and systems of government, it has survived both republics and empires; the art of making pottery, the woven baskets, the musical instruments depicted in the frescoes of Bonampak have survived Mayan high priests, Aztec warriors, Spanish friars and Mexican presidents. These arts will also survive Yankee tourists. Craftsmen have no fatherland; their roots are in their native village—or even in just one quarter of it, or within their own families."*

Despite the philosopher's faith in the lasting qualities of the hand arts of his country, and the effective life-saving measures being taken by the Mexican government, it is apparent already that some folk arts have disappeared or are declining in quality, and that others may not survive this century.

Much has been written (mostly in Spanish) about the major popular arts of Mexico—weaving, pottery, lacquer and basketry. Very little has been written (and almost nothing in English) about the simpler crafts and rare ceremonial pieces that are the subject of this book.

In spite of our hope that the hand arts of Mexico will remain purely Indian and will live on unaffected by modern development or Yankee tourists, it is the question of their survival that gave impetus to the preparation of our book. The objects were collected between 1967 and 1977 and photographed *just in case* some of them might disappear. Of course, a book cannot bring about the salvation of a single lost skill or object, and it can capture only a two-dimensional portrait of the small but wonderfully decorative things that face an uncertain future. So, while there is still time, here is a little-known but *picante* portion of the flavor and color of Mexico.

*Paz; introduction to *In Praise of Hands*, page 23.

Pair of carefully-dressed little rag dolls; the man carries two small drums and wears a hat woven of *ixtle* fiber; the woman carries a small clay pot; embroidered faces. 4¾″ tall (12.1 cm.) *Gift of Yvonne Forbath.*

12

I

THE TOYS OF MEXICO

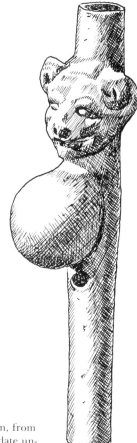

Clay whistle, probably Mayan, from Jaina, Campeche, Yucatán; date unknown. Length 6½" (16.5 cm.).

SILENTLY AT REST in the sandy earth of Mexico for many hundreds of years were the remains of early Indian civilizations—the oldest dating as far back as 1500 B. C. The native Indians of the country served scores of emperors during those passing years, pursuing the tasks of their agricultural society; they were largely ignorant of the nature of the lives of their ancestors, and of the extent of their own heritage.

In the year 1519 Hernando Cortes landed in Vera Cruz with a small, ruthless Spanish army, seeking gold for the crown of Spain. From that date, the destiny of Mexico changed completely in a few brief years.

Soon after the swift conquest of Mexico, Spanish scholars arrived in New Spain and began to take an interest in the past of their new colony. They found its history to be quite different from their own. While warriors and adventurers were seeking wealth, the professors and historians began investigations that proved to be a fascinating study.

Later, over a period of years in the 18th and 19th centuries, the Spanish Viceroys granted freedom of passage to various European scientists and engineers who financed their own small New World expeditions. They explored Mexico's abandoned and half-hidden pyramids and ceremonial centers. There were artists in some of these exploring parties who recorded what they saw, and eventually several books were published in Europe illustrating for the first time the marvels of ancient Mexican Indian artifacts, architecture and sculpture. It was not until after Mexico had achieved its independence in 1910 that the Mexican government was in a position to undertake systematic studies of its own archeological treasures.

Toys in Mexican History

Burial sites believed to date from about 1 A. D. have yielded tools, weapons and pottery pieces, and also some toy-like objects that at first were thought to be children's playthings. Fired pottery balls, whistles and small animal figures on wheels which appeared to be pull-toys were unearthed at Tres Zapotes, Las Tuxtlas in Vera Cruz on the east coast of Mexico. Other such wheeled pieces were found in Central Mexico.

The wheeled toys are especially puzzling to scientists and historians because there is no evidence

13

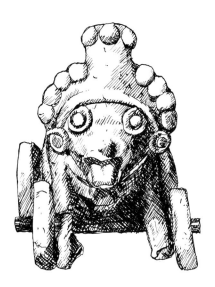

Wheeled pottery animal with crown; wheels were usually found separately, but there were holes for axles through the feet of the animal. Date unknown—possibly the first or second century A. D. Height about 6″, length 7″ (15.2 × 17.8 cm.).

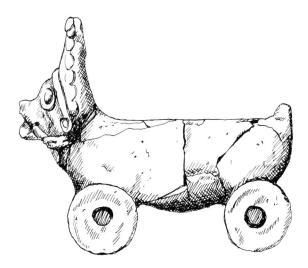

that the wheel was known or used in early Central American civilizations. The puzzle is not yet completely solved: were these toys, how did they come to have wheels, or what were they?

A comprehensive study of tomb findings was completed in 1950 by a Mexican scholar, Francisco Javier Hernandez, who finally concluded that such objects as fired clay balls, whistles, wheeled dogs and other animals were probably made expressly to be used as funereal offerings or votive figures to be buried with the adult dead of high rank, but that they were not children's playthings. He cites the fact that such unearthed objects appear never to have been used and are in perfect condition. Furthermore, no toys are described or pictured in Mexican codices— the 16th century history books with many illustrations of various phases of Mexican life. Hernandez' opinion is now widely accepted.*

Daniel Rubin de la Borbolla, former director of the Museum of Popular Arts in Mexico City says that the most antique clay toys are the whistles of Oaxaca, Puebla, Tonalá and Tlaquepaque. Other very old toys are the clay turtles—which are usually rattles or whistles—wood, clay and papier mâché dolls, rattles made of woven palm and miniature musical instruments.

Indians and Indian children all over Mexico have always devised toys of their own making, and these must surely be included among the early historic toys of the country. They are not very different from country Indian toys of today— bamboo whistles, reed darts, corn cob and corn shuck dolls, horses made of twigs, rag dolls and toys made of rope, straw and palm leaves.

Colonial Mexico

By the latter part of the 17th century the Spanish had brought not only their laws, language and religion to Mexico, but the whole social life of New Spain—especially in the cities—was Spanish in dress and customs, for those who could afford it. Indians and country people, although ostensibly religious converts, kept to their own customs, lived simply and knew nothing of the way of life in prosperous cities and in the new royal court of Mexico City. Children of colonial Mexico played games and sang songs imported from Spain, to accompany the boys' war games and the girls' game of playing house. By 1800 ships from Europe had begun to bring all kinds of goods including beautifully-printed board games,

*El Juguete Popular en Mexico; Estudio de Interpretacion Ediciones Mexicanas, S. A., Mexico, 19509, Vol. 10.

and the well-to-do children of Mexico played gambling, bull-fight and circus games from Spain. Dolls, doll houses, wind-up animals, and puppet theaters came from Germany and Austria. Kites and aerial balloons became favorite diversions of *muchachos* who enjoyed good flying weather and blue skies almost all year round. Christmas crèche figures from France and Italy were the elegant ancestors of Mexico's wax, clay and wood *nacimiento* figures. Lead soldiers, miniatures and paper dolls came from abroad too, and Mexican children treasured this whole parade of toys like many other children of the times everywhere in the western world.*

The Twentieth Century

Whatever is distinctive about playthings in this sunny country is due to the special character and guileless philosophy of the artisans who make them. These qualities have remained the same throughout many years. In 1928, René d'Harnoncourt, an American museum curator who loved Mexico, wrote his impression of the native toymaker, and that perceptive and charming picture is still descriptive:

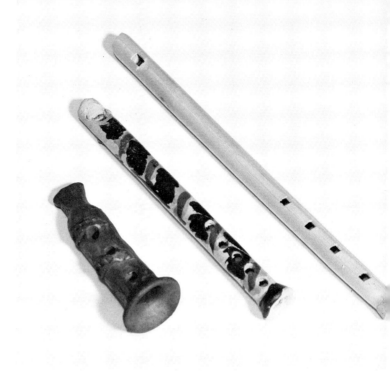

Three flutes or whistles; left to right, black clay, tempera-painted clay and reed; these are toys of very old Indian tradition. Length: 4″, 7″ and 9¾″ (10.2, 17.8 and 24.8 cm.)

PANCHO THE TOYMAKER

"The toymaker's customers are the Indians who never outgrow their desire for something to play with. In no other country would the peasant population devote so much time to selection, and spend so much money on the purchase of a purely esthetic object. The toy may be graceful, funny or grotesque, but as long as it stimulates the imagination, it fulfills the only purpose of a perfect toy.

"Neither the toymaker or his clients take his efforts toward efficiency very seriously. He makes fancy piggybanks but they are often too small to hold a centavo. The slot in the larger banks is too narrow to pass a coin. His miniature water pitchers do not pour. Most of the toymaker's animal creations demonstrate his unique sense of humor. Pancho considers himself free to fashion a quaint world after his own will and fancy.

"The opportunity to sell his own wares in the market and at a fiesta when toys are bought and the atmosphere is gay, means more to the toymaker than just a certain amount of cash. It is impossible to persuade him to sell his merchandise on the way to the market.

"Pancho and his art are not really children of the twentieth century. He is often unconscious of the merit of his own work and is inclined to admire the commercial productions of a 'superior' civilization. Pancho may live in misery, he may be the victim of disease, but in his work he follows his own will and pleasures, and if only his most

elemental needs are satisfied for the moment, he is the most contented being on earth. We see him wandering on all the highways of Mexico, bargaining on all the plazas, and smiling behind his stand at every street corner. We most fervently hope that we shall never lose him and his playthings—the most charming souvenirs of a time of delightful inefficiency."*

Mexican Folkways, Vol. 4, No. 2, April-June, 1928.

"Pancho the Toymaker" with his display of doll furniture at the market at Ocotlán, Oaxaca.

Lo Efímero y Eterno del Arte Popular Mexicano, page 20— (author's translation.)

15

Mold-cast pottery siren with guitar; painted pink, green, white, black and gold, varnished. Height 4¾″ (12.1 cm.)

During the years when imported toys filled the playtime needs of wealthy youngsters, native artisans kept on making their clay, wood, straw, reed, palm and tin objects and simple toys. Craftspeople in widespread areas of Mexico produced distinctive styles of work; over the years certain clays and other locally available natural materials were utilized to produce unique objects of ingenuous design and color. Toys made in Oaxaca, for instance, were recognizably different from the clay toys of other pottery centers. Olinalá became known for the excellence of its lacquer work. Mexican craftsmen followed the traditions of their village predecessors in making what are now defined as *folk art* objects, many of which had fine esthetic qualities as well as their utilitarian character.

One of the first people to recognize the importance of the popular arts of his country was Gerardo Murillo, known as *Dr. Atl.* He was a man of wide-ranging interests—an artist, writer, photographer, critic, city planner, labor organizer and founder of the National Academy (of arts). Dr. Atl was one of the first to write about native folk arts and to photograph them for his two-volume book, *Las Artes Populares en Mexico,* published in 1922. The book attracted great attention at the time and the excellent text is still considered to be highly authoritative.

Whistle, pottery devil painted with red and black tempera colors and varnished. Height 4″ (10.2 cm.) *Gift of Yvonne Forbath.*

Fifty years have gone by since the time of that Pancho. Mexican toymakers who carry their own wares around on foot and set up their rickety little stalls along city streets have indeed almost been lost, and are seen much less often nowadays. In the parks of Mexico City, the busiest vendors of today are the balloon men and those who sell factory-made plastic rockets and pink airplanes launched by a wind-up spring. But the same modest makers of hand-made toys still exist in considerable numbers, and can be found in the streets of smaller towns and villages and at Indian markets.

No fiesta or religious celebration is complete, even now, without the toys made especially for it, and at festival time Pancho reappears year after year. He keeps on making his wares and Mexican families continue to buy them. The toymaker differs from many Mexicans because his destiny is clear before him. Thus freed from uncertainty and confident of his skills, however modest, he finds a secure and special place in the everyday life of his country.

Carved wood armadillo made of copal wood, left its natural
white; tail and four legs attached by small nails; decorated
with a black felt pen. Length 6½″ (16.5 cm.)

Like many Mexicans living in the new republic—after the Spanish government was over-
thrown in 1910—Murillo did not like the idea of
being mistaken for a Spaniard because of his His-
panic name. So he called himself *Dr. Atl,* a word
spelled like the last syllable of many Náhuatl words in
the language of the Aztecs, and made up of a
combination of letters that many Spanish could not
pronounce. He felt that his assumed name identified
him as being purely Mexican, and it was always used
by his colleagues.

Dr. Atl was a rebel and the Academy he established was non-conformist both artistically and politi-
cally. Very few of the early twentieth century Mexican painters were of pure Indian blood, but their
association as artists manifested itself in a rejection of
European styles and the adoption of simpler native
Mexican values. Later another organization was
formed called "The Revolutionary Syndicate of
Technical Workers, Painters and Sculptors" and it
allied itself strongly with the laboring people.* Many
of the drawings, paintings and frescoes of Merida,
Rivera, Orozco, Siqueiros, Goitia, Fonserrada and
Tamayo use themes that are sociological, historical
and political, while stylistically they are all strongly
Mexican.

*Brenner, p. 231

Dr. Atl considered the popular arts to be one of
the most important manifestations of the distinctive
qualities of a people. The popular or folk arts include
such handcrafts as pottery, weaving, lacquer work,
basketry, carving and various ritual, decorative and
miniature objects. Atl said, "In studying the folk arts
it is possible to evaluate with great precision certain
qualities of a race. What are those qualities that are
revealed to us by a study of the popular arts of
Mexico? They are these: great artistic feeling—
especially a strong decorative feeling—enormous
physical endurance, an individualistic spirit that
transforms and organizes everything that is assimi-
lated, giving it a personal stamp, an admirable
manual ability and great fantasy."* Dr. Atl wrote in
his own book "I affirm categorically that the indigenous arts of any country cannot be tampered with.
They are a product of such a distinctive style, so
intimately tied to the idiosyncracies of their produc-
ers that to touch them is to destroy them. Popular arts
are those which spring spontaneously from a people
as an immediate consequence of their family, civil or
religious needs. When they are cultivated under an
artistic or commercial influence foreign to those
needs, they cease to be truly popular arts."**

La Efimero y Eterno del Arte Popular Mexicano, page 20—
(author's translation.)

**Murillo, Vol. I, page 45. (author's translation.)

Pecking bird, a traditional moving toy that works by a small clay ball swung from a string, making the bird's tail move up and down as the bird pecks for food in a tiny acorn cup. Partly painted in magenta and green. Bird is 2⅞″ long (7.3 cm.)

Snake and turtle in confrontation; snake decorated with aniline colors, and articulated with string; turtle made of copal wood, unpainted. Snake 12¼″ long, turtle 4¹/₁₆″ (31.1 and 10.3 cm.)

Dr. Atl's evaluation of the art of the common man in Mexico may not seem very remarkable to people living in the last quarter of the twentieth century, but it must be recognized that the view of the popular arts has undergone considerable change in fifty years and such arts have gradually acquired increased interest and importance. All folk arts—European, African, South Sea and those of South and North American Indians are now apt to be equated with other arts for their charm, individuality and sociological and historical importance.

Atl's perceptive and articulate appraisal of objects that may have seemed to others to be commonplace and almost worthless artistically in 1922 was prophetically ahead of its time. Mexican popular arts today, or those that have not been "tampered with", occupy a unique place in a world that is more universally aware of the significance and wide range of the arts. Folk toys occupy an important niche in the gallery of popular arts in modern Mexico.

Richard Grove, an American museum curator, gives us a poetic picture of the ambience of Mexican arts. He says, "We are reminded over and over again that many of the things are made today the way they were hundreds of years ago, assuming final form, realizing to the last degree the nature of their simple materials. This can be an eerie sensation because Mexican time is not arranged conveniently and reassuringly into succeeding years and centuries. The centuries refuse to die but instead go on shuffling uneasily through the backlands like old men who have retired to their homes."*

*Introduction to *Mexican Popular Arts Today;* The Taylor Museum of the Colorado Springs Fine Arts Center, Colorado Springs, Colorado, 1954.

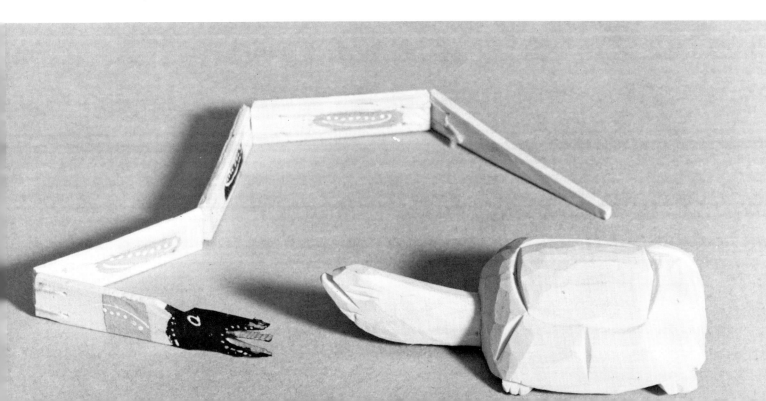

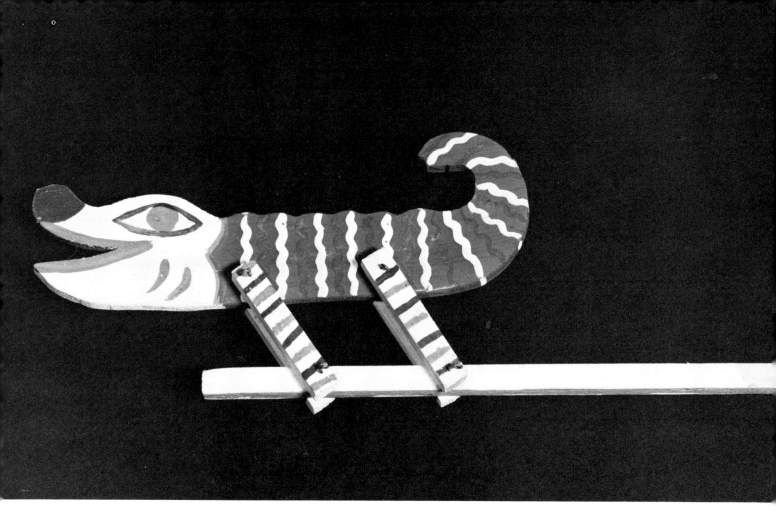

Crocodile, painted wood jump-toy; white, red, blue and green. Legs articulated with nails; toy is held tightly in one hand, and when the stick is hit sharply, the crocodile jumps forward, then backward. Length of figure 7½″ (19.1 cm.) *Gift of Stephen Forbath.*

Black pottery turtle whistle; the tail is a whistle with a low, mournful sound; the clay surface was burnished with a stone before one firing in the kiln. Made at San Bartólo Coyotepec, Oaxaca in the studio of one of Mexico's most famous potters—Doña Rosa. Length 6¼″ (15.9 cm.)

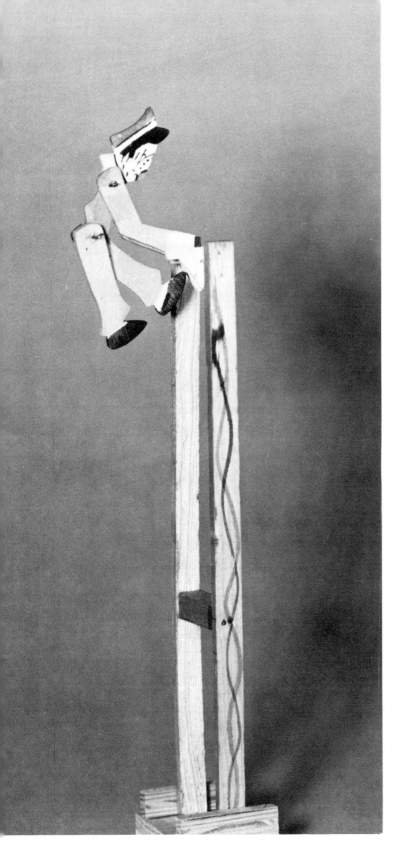

Clown jumping jack, partly-painted wood.
Figure 5½″ (14 cm.)

Crocodile jumping jack, partly-painted wood.
Figure 5½″ long (14 cm.)

Rattle woven of dyed and natural palm leaf—green and red, filled with small metal bells and decorated with feathers. Length 8″ (20.3 cm.)

Three men made of woven palm leaf—two carrying pineapples and one playing a horn; natural color with touches of red and green. Height 3¼″ (8.3 cm.)

Child's rattle woven of dyed and natural palm leaf—partly colored in red and green; filled with gourd seeds. Length 10″ (25.4 cm.)

22

Deer made of palm leaf strips—natural and dyed green.
4½″ × 5″ (11.4 × 12.7 cm.)

Mouse made of palm leaf strips, woven and twisted, natural
color. Length without tail 2½″ (6.4 cm.)

Mexico Today

The world of Mexican folk toys is larger, more varied, more inventive, more humorous, more colorful and more imaginative than the toy world of any other country. The photographs here can be seen as a strong affirmation of this rather extravagant statement. Mexican folk toys are also simpler, less expensive, less often mechanized, less elegant, less pretentious and less contrived than others.

The playthings of Mexico are not designed under the guidance of a child psychologist and are not efficiently made in a factory by the thousands in such a way that they will not break, chip, fade or hurt anybody. They are never boxed with a book of instructions, and in Mexico, toys positively will not last forever, and some may not even last a week.

Most Mexican toys are handmade by Indian or Mexican-Indian artisans at their own whim and at a pace of their own choice. Toys are made principally for youngsters—who are quickly responsive to them, and only incidentally for grown-ups who are charmed by them. The artisan may live and work in a simple adobe house in the country, or in a small, painted stucco dwelling like dozens of others strung along a dusty city street. The craftsman's house is seldom identified or differentiated from the neighbor's house by even the smallest sign. Such toymakers exist and work in comparative anonymity in all parts of the country.

The Mexican toymaker loves children and usually has four or five of his own. He sometimes devises a new toy, but is more likely to make several that are more or less alike, in exactly the way his father taught him to make them. When a craftsman invents a new toy, it is sometimes as much for his own amusement as for a child. If his craft is pottery or papier mâché, it is quite probable that he presses his material into the same mold that his grandfather used for making a small animal or doll. The toymaker knows that all children break playthings and that youngsters tire of toys—except the one or two that become battered favorites. Accordingly, he uses simple tools to put his pieces of wood together with nails or wires that are not concealed, uses the cheapest clay, wood, tin and paper he can find, and sometimes splashes on bright colors with a home-made brush in a most casual way. However, if a painted decoration is a traditional feature of a toy, the painting is done with great skill. A potter knows his craft well, but he is apt to stick clay arms and legs on a little doll without being very particular about how they look.

Opposite page: A stylized representation in woven wheat straw of the Arms of the Republic of Mexico. The symbol is a representation of an eagle perching on a cactus, devouring a serpent, and was taken from a glyph representing the Aztec city of Tenochtitlan (now Mexico City).

Boxers—natural wood partly painted in red, green and black aniline colors. A flat piece of (salvaged) spring steel in the base is pressed down with the knob in the center, making the boxers lean toward each other with arms swinging. Made in Salamanca, Guanajuato. Base 6″ long (15.2 cm.)

Horse and cowboy jumping jack partly painted in black, white, red and green; head made of painted clay; articulated with nails and cords and shown in extended position. Width 6¾″ (17.1 cm.)

If a spirit of play and a sort of irrational sense of fun are to be seen in the toys of any country, they are seen clearly in those of Mexico. If the wonder and silliness of miniatures is felt and understood anywhere, it is almost a love-cult in Mexico. If the rare human expression of pure joy can be seen anywhere, it is on the faces of men, women and children watching Mexican fireworks.

The Spanish word for Toy Shop is *Juguetería,* but such a sign is seldom seen in Mexico because toys are found among the wares of many kinds of shops; these may be identified by the family name of the owner, or by a first name: *La Inez,* or simply *La Tienda*—The Store. Toys may stand on a corner shelf, or be jumbled together in a basket on the floor, or they may be hanging overhead or scattered about on a counter among more impressive goods. Toys are also seen in Indian market *puestos,* or in a basket on a vendor's back in public parks on a week-end or holiday. At festival time, toy stalls blossom everywhere, springing up as a colorful and integral part of the celebration. Toys for special occasions may be seen for only a few days during the festivities, and cannot be found easily at any other time. In a very special way, toys mark almost every occasion upon which a Mexican has something to celebrate, and that happens very often.

Merry-go-round or flying swing (*volantín*) made of pottery painted with tempera colors: white, purple, green and pink. The umbrella-like top is a separate piece with tiny figures hanging from wires around its edge; this balances on the tip of the post, and is twirled by hand to give the people a ride. This is a very old and always primitively-made toy. Height 5″ (12.7 cm.)

Airplane made of wheat straw (*panicua*) in natural color with wheels and propeller attached by common pins. Made in Tzintzuntzán, Michoacán. Length 10″ (25.4 cm.)

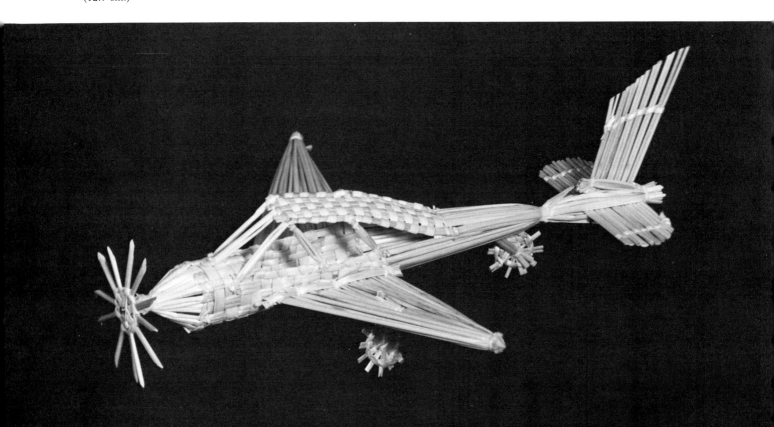

Bull, primitively carved and painted copal wood, colored
with aniline magenta and black india ink. Made by a
farmer-grandfather, Zinpe Fuente in San Martin Tilcajete,
Oaxaca. Length 15″, height 9¼″ (38.1 × 23.5 cm.)

Wooden toy gun—a slingshot with a lever release for the
elastic-propelled stone or pellet. Partly painted with aniline
colors in red and green. Length 17½″ (44.5 cm.)

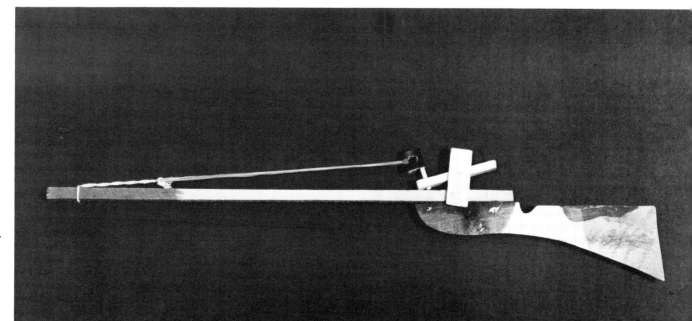

Two owls and a bird, pottery burnished and decorated by brush; earth color with dark and red-brown decoration. Made in the studio of Jorge Wilmot at Tonalá, Chiapas. Owls 2¾″ and 1½″ tall, bird 2⅛″ tall (7 and 3.8; 5.4 cm.)

Animal musicians, hand-made green-glazed pottery with each fantastic creature playing a different instrument. This exotic musical group is produced in Santa María Atzompa, Oaxaca and is not made elsewhere (unless perhaps imitated.) The group is made in several sizes, from one very tiny one and is sometimes made of unglazed buff clay and more usually glazed with the village's distinctive green glaze. Children as young as seven years of age model the musicians—all of which are formed by hand, and therefore there are never two figures exactly alike. Height 3″ to 3¼″ (7.6 to 8.3 cm.)

Two partly-painted wood pull toys: lion and cowboy on a horse; colors red, green, black. Length 3½″ and 3¾″ (8.9 and 9.5 cm.)

Top with holder and cord—painted wood, partly lathe-turned; modern version of an age-old toy. Diameter of top 3″ (7.6 cm.)

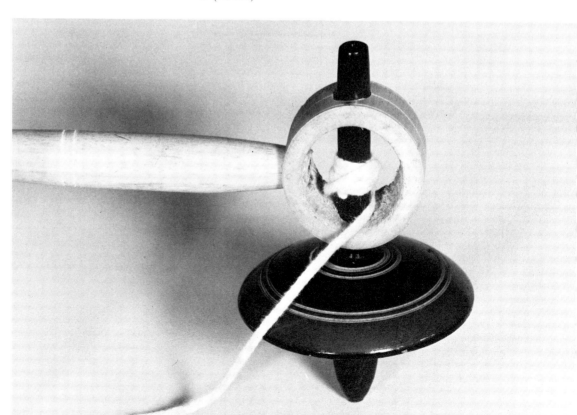

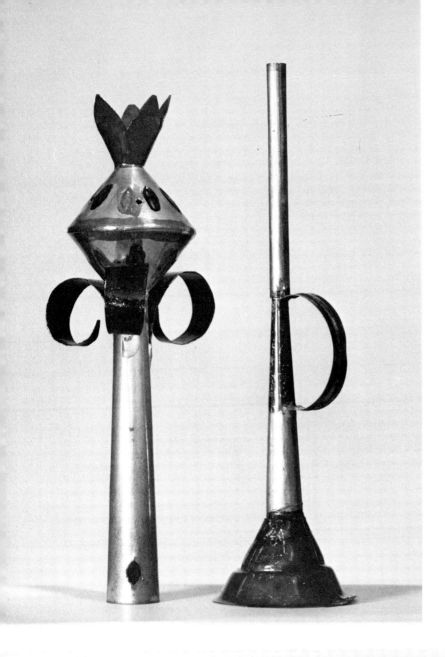

Tin rattle and horn, painted with red and blue enamel;
Rattle based on Indian dance rattle design. Rattle 7¼″ long,
horn 7¾″ (18.4 - 19.7 cm.)

Cup and ball toy—painted wood—a modern lathe-turned
version of a colonial toy. The object of the game is to toss the
ball (barrel) and catch it on the stick. Barrel 2¾″ long (7 cm.)

Doll, mold-pressed papier maché, painted blue, pink, red, white, black; looking slightly cross-eyed and sitting on a spool of thread. Height 5½″ (14 cm.)

Pottery piggy-bank and whistle animal (bird-pig?) painted with pink and white tempera paints, varnished. A dual-purpose and dual-form toy. Height 5″ (12.7 cm.)

31

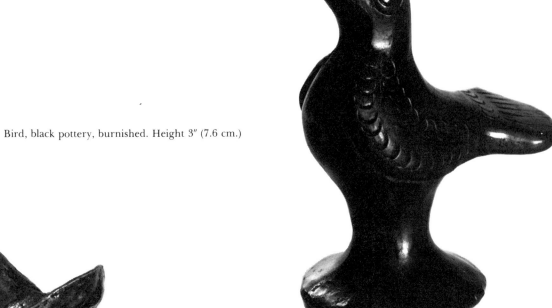

Bird, black pottery, burnished. Height 3″ (7.6 cm.)

Chesspiece—Knight—papier maché mold-pressed figure with hat, blanket-roll and "ropes" added. Painted tan, brown, blue, black and gold and varnished. Height 6½″ (16.5 cm.) Made by Guadalupe Rodriguez, San Miguel de Allende, Guanajuato.

Corpus Christi *mulito,* the traditional toy made for the June
festival honoring the arrival of the first fruits of the season
in Mexico. The legs, ears and crates are made of broomcorn
stalks; the body is stuffed with straw, covered with corn
shucks (sometimes banana leaves) tied with twisted grasses
and painted with aniline colors. Length 7″, height 10¼″
(17.8 × 26 cm.) *Gift of Carlos Espejel.*

One-wire puppet with painted clay head, hands and feet which are glued onto the cloth costume decorated with foil and feathers. These inexpensive little toys come dressed in many different costumes and are used in dramatic productions in home-made paper theaters. A stiff wire is attached to the puppet's head, and the figures can be moved up and down to perform a very animated dance. Height 8¼″ (21 cm.)

Miniature baskets made of natural and dyed split palm leaf. The larger size is often used ceremonially to hold candles or food for grave offerings on the Day of the Dead. Height 1¾″, 2″ and 3½″ (4.4, 5.1 and 8.9 cm.)

Bird with big feet and a haughty stance; carved wood painted with aniline colors. Height 5″ (12.7 cm.)

A menacing beast carved of copal wood, painted with aniline colors and firmly put together with two sizes of nails. 7″ × 3¾″ (17.8 × 9.5 cm.)

Crocodile—jointed pull-toy made of wood cut with a jigsaw and painted with aniline colors; the two body sections are loosely joined by salvaged blue-steel strapping. The crocodile swims a very wavy course when pulled. Length 10½″, height 2¾″ (26.7 × 7 cm.)

Giraffe (*jirafa*) carved and painted by Manuel Jiménez. The back legs seem to be nailed on at the wrong angle, and the spots are round, but the animal's stance is firm, and he could not be mistaken for any other creature. Length 9¼″, height 10¾″ (23.5 × 27.3 cm.)

Ferris Wheel, *Rueda de Fortuna* or Wheel of Fortune; wood and wire construction painted with aniline colors. Each little chair holds a rider and when the wheel is turned by the crank, the chairs swing loosely on copper wire and stay upright during the ride. Made by Felipe Gomez and his children, Oaxaca City. Length 15⅝″, height 10″ (39.7 × 25.4 cm.) Riders are 3″ tall (7.6 cm.)

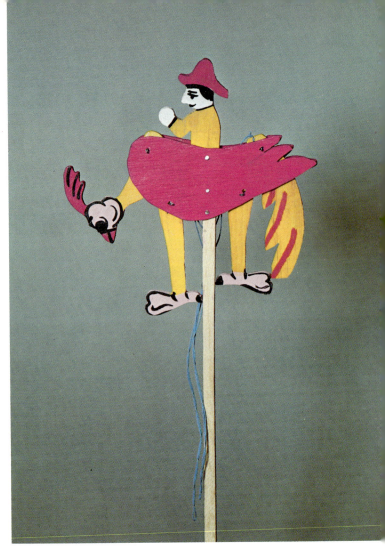

Man riding on a galloping ostrich—painted wood jumping jack operated by pulling a cord. Width, extended 9½″, height 6″ (24.1 × 15.2 cm.)

Man seated on a tired ostrich—jumping jack.

Cock fight—two feathered roosters with bodies made of tissue paper stuffed with cotton; legs and beaks of real quills. Long wires can be stuck into the bodies of the cocks so that two children can stage a lively fight. Length 5″ from beak to tail (12.7 cm.)

Angry armadillo—carved wood, painted with aniline colors; tail, feet and head attached by nails. A drab and common Mexican animal as seen in glorious colors by Manual Jiménez. Length 19″, height 3¼″ (48.3 × 8.3 cm.)

Camel, mold-made papier maché, painted with tempera colors; the pose is a typically Mexican touch. Length 7¾″, height 8¼″ (19.7 × 21 cm.)

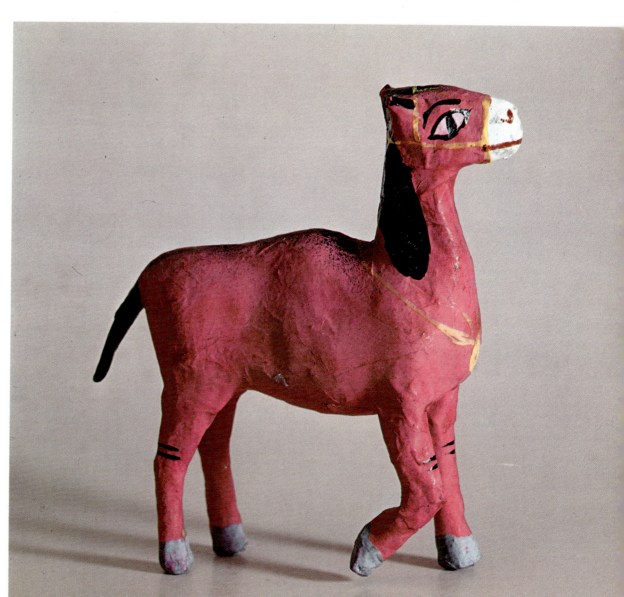

A miniature replica of the tiger mask worn in carnivals and for the Dance of the Tigers—depicting worship of the sacred jaguar. Carved wood with paper ears and tongue, painted in enamels. Boar bristles are used for fierce eyebrows and whiskers. 1¾" × 3" (4.4 × 7.6 cm.)

Leopard couchant, but wide awake; painted wood by Jiménez of Arrasola. Length 9¾", height 2⅛" (24.8 × 5.4 cm.)

Seven-year-old weaver at Santo Tomás Jalieza, Oaxaca.

The Mexican Family

While Mexican children accept responsibilities that make them seem very adult at the age of seven or eight, the grown-ups have many child-like qualities that they never seem to outgrow. Men and women love sweets, delight in occasional noise and horseplay, dance untiringly at a fiesta and favor brightly-colored clothing and decorations. Mexicans from 8 to 80 buy almost a million and a half comic books per week at about 10¢ per copy.

All members of a family enter into simple diversions together and enjoy the pleasure of games and celebrations. Babies in arms are wrapped in the mother's *rebozo* and kept up late with the older children to share the color and fun of a festival. Children also participate solemnly in religious processions, pageants, pastoral plays and *posadas*—sometimes taking a more important rôle than their elders. Family ties are very strong in Mexico.

In a household where the father is a craftsman such as a toymaker or weaver, or if the mother is a potter (largely a woman's craft) the children begin to learn the family trade at the age of six or seven. It is not at all unusual to find a family of six or eight: parents, sons and daughters, cousins and grandparents working together in a home workshop—which is often the whole house—to produce folk crafts of a particular kind. In this way, handcraft skills have been passed from one generation to the next for many years, and the traditional shapes, colors and patterns of the craft change very little. An inventive artisan may occasionally add his own touches to a piece of work so that some new and distinctive details appear now and then, but on the whole there is not much inclination to change the nature of established crafts.

Generalizations about the character of the people of any nation are never wholly acceptable, and certainly cannot be made by foreigners. Octavio Paz, the Mexican philosopher, who has made a deeply serious study of his fellow-countrymen and the nature of their lives gives his book a poetically descriptive title: *The Labyrinth of Solitude*. The Mexican family has many distinctive qualities, and if the adults do seem solitary or lost in a quiet diffidence at times, they also clearly have an endearing capacity for explosive gaiety when the occasion is an auspicious one.

Mexican boys and girls, especially among country people and Indians, have fewer years of carefree childhood than most other twentieth century youngsters. By the time they are about eight years old, they are expected to do their share of farm and household chores. Boys care for animals and carry heavy containers of water. Girls help with the cooking, cleaning and laundry, tend the baby and walk long distances carrying baskets or bags of provisions. Indian country children often dress in clothes like those worn by their parents—long skirts and *rebozos* for the girls and long pants and a straw hat for boys; bright colored shirts and sweaters are favored by everybody. The young people look like little grown-ups at a very tender age.

City children wear clothes like youngsters in many other countries, and when they start to school they usually wear neat little uniforms. Mexican teen-age girls like short skirts and slacks and boys follow current hair styles. Mexicans of all classes are proud and devoted parents and indulge their children when they are very young; the children seem to respond by performing the duties that are expected of them with affectionate compliance. Young people in general are shy or respectful with strangers and very well-behaved in public.

Games Children Play

Frances Toor, an expert on folk customs tells an authoritative story of the games played by Mexican Indian youngsters.

"The native children of primitive communities of today are undoubtedly playing the same games as those played by their ancestors before the Conquest—taught them by their elders or perhaps they are imitations of the elders' sports and pastimes. As a rule there are no commercial toys available in those regions; if there were, their parents could not afford to buy them, so the children create their own play world and take advantage of what their environment has to offer.

"Tarahuama Indian boys—whose parents raise cattle—carve hoofs of horses, burros and sheep on the ends of sticks with which they jump along to make tracks on soft earth. They also carve animal heads from branches, add small twigs for horns and play at bullfighting. From pine twigs they make traps for animals, canoes, corrals with tiny animals, toy plows, wagons and horses.

"Tarahuama girls play at housekeeping and make mud *tortillas* and are clever at making dolls of plants and sticks dressed in flowers and weeds. Both boys and girls enjoy imitating their elders' drinking feasts, so they pretend to serve corn beer to their dolls in acorn cups until they get them drunk and make them behave as their parents do on such occasions.

"Maya Indian boys make pellet guns of plants, cane whistles, palm leaf trumpets and sling shots of rubber or sisal fiber. Children extract a liquid from shoots of a plant called *pomolche,* and make bubbles by blowing the juice through tin tubes.

"Boys everywhere play at marbles, bullfighting, lassoing bulls and spinning tops which they make themselves. During the apricot season, the boys play a game called *huesitos,* or "little bones" with the stones of the fruit. A hole is dug in the ground just big enough to hold one stone; the boys take turns throwing their stones at the hole from a certain distance and the one whose stone falls into the hole wins all the stones around it. Boys are also fond of playing *policia y ladrones*—cops and robbers—and at pretending army maneuvers with wooden guns."*

*Toor, *Mexican Folkways,* p. 261 ff.

Mexican children play all kinds of games while they sing songs that are often quite funny—games like London Bridge is Falling Down and Musical Chairs. Many of their songs and chants have very old Spanish origins and came from Andalusia.

All these Mexican-flavored games prove that the Encyclopedia Britannica would be entirely right if it also said that children's games have changed very little over the centuries.

Modernization

In Mexico City one may occasionally see an Indian craftsman who has come in from the country by bus carrying a cotton bag full of his carvings or other hand-made objects. He shows his work to the owner of a shop, and if it is acceptable, he is paid what may seem to us to be a small amount of money for the whole lot.

The modernization of Mexican cities is a looming threat to the artisan traditions, now that plastic toys, synthetic yarns and dyes and metal kitchenware and other manufactured accessories are commonly available. Bright-hued plastics are seen everywhere, and since they are cheap and attractive to people who love color, they are slowly replacing many of the charming indigenous wood, clay, reed and straw objects of the country. The latter are beginning to be regarded as old fashioned by the natives.

The production of a number of traditional Mexican handcrafts continues in many places because of the sustained tourist market for them. It is still possible for a visitor to find traditional folk arts in shops—especially in larger cities in gallery-shops, even though such pieces are no longer to be found in native markets. It takes some knowledge and a sharp eye to find good traditional toys and other craft pieces among the profusion of wares and mass-produced trinkets for sale in the many small shops geared to the tourist trade.

The government and state-sponsored folk art museums and shops scattered throughout Mexico in the larger cities are keeping many of the traditional handcrafts alive and we owe them a debt of thanks that some of the charming things of the country that might otherwise have disappeared continue to be made for our enjoyment. (List at end of Chapter VI).

Little girls weaving cotton belts at Santo Tomás Jalieza, Oaxaca.

Maria Teresa Pomar is one of the most knowledgeable people in Mexico about the popular arts of her country. She is (1977) director of the Museo Nacional de Artes e Industrias Populares in Mexico City, and she reassures us about the future of her country's folk arts, saying: "I believe we can count on the good taste of the masses. The villagers are less taken by plastic objects than most people think. Some years ago a thousand wooden toys handcrafted in Guanajuato were offered for sale at a fair in Michoacán, side by side with plastic toys. There were more customers for the wooden toys than for their plastic competitors. The villagers remain the best customers for Mexican handcrafted wares despite the export of several million dollars' worth each year. Don't you agree this is a good reason for optimism?"*

*National Geographic, May, 1978: *Mexican Folk Arts,* p. 669

Summary

The character of Mexican toys—their variety, simplicity and lively inventiveness—has its origin in the heritage and character of the Indians of Mexico. The folk toys did not take on the flavor of Spanish arts and they continue to have a spirit of fantasy and naive play about them that is seldom seen in sophisticated societies.

The folk *arts* of Mexico have received much attention in recent years, but any sort of review or catalog has a tendency to pass over folk *toys* very lightly. Yet the toy world of Mexico is unfailingly distinctive, and in a group of playthings from around the world, the Mexican pieces would probably be the most easily identifiable.

It is to be hoped that twentieth century influences cannot change or dim the glow of the bright toys of Mexico any more than the elegance of Spanish baroque design changed them more than three hundred years ago.

Coyote, carved and painted copal wood—aniline colors:
orange body, red ears and black spots. The ears and tail are
stuck into carved holes in the body and the legs are attached
by small black-headed nails. Made by Manuel Jiménez,
master carver of Arrasola, Oaxaca. Length 12¾″, height 6¼″
(32.4 × 15.9 cm.)

Lizard-like animal candle holder, fired clay painted with
tempera in light and dark brown. Length 5⅜″ (13.7 cm.)

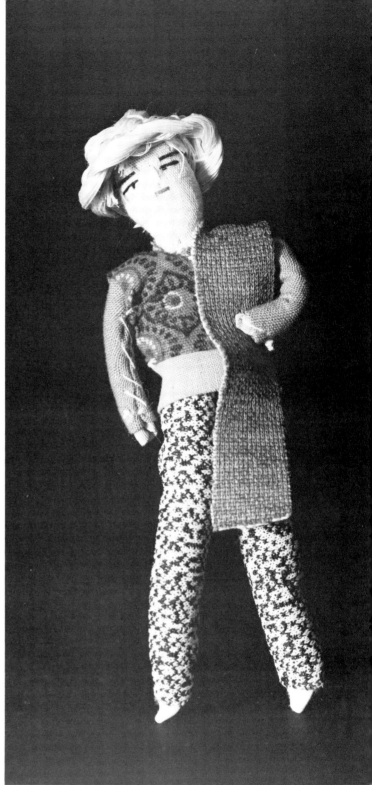

Clown that squeaks (*payaso con fuelle*); toy on a stick—small bellows inside the body make the clown squeak when he is shaken. Painted clay head, cloth suit. Height of figure 6″ (15.2 cm.)

Rag doll—man in hat woven of *ixtle* fiber and wearing a *serape*. Height 4¾″ (12.1 cm.)

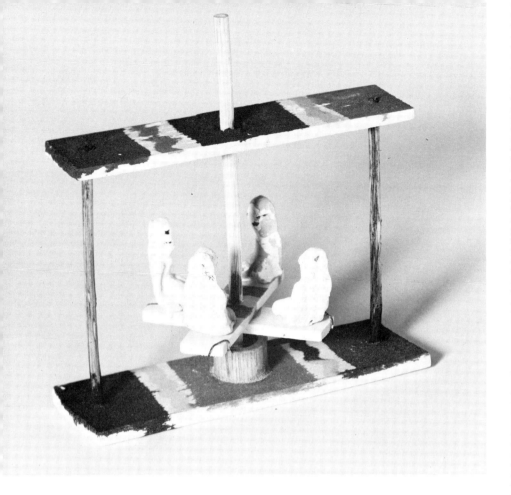

Merry-go-round toy, painted wood and clay; to give the little clay figures a ride, the stick is twirled by the top; painted pink, purple and yellow. 5″ × 4″ (12.7 × 10.2 cm.)

Butterfly push-toy, painted tin and wire on wooden stick. The wings are painted with enamel—green with black and white spots. When the wheels turn, the butterfly slowly flaps its wings. Height 4½″, wingspread 8″ (11.4 × 20.3 cm.)

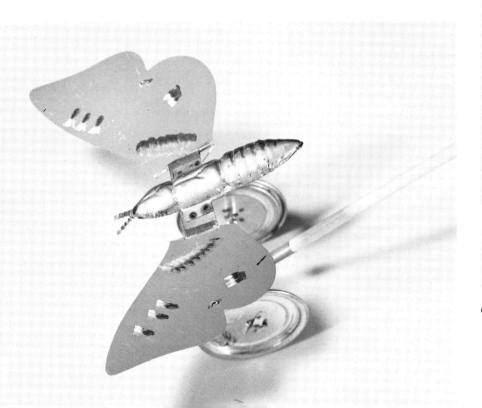

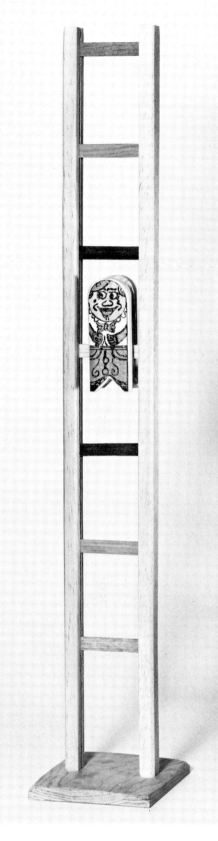

Acrobat who comes down a ladder; painted wood. The figure is slotted in such a way that when it is started at the top, it flip-flops down the ladder and lands on its feet; multicolors. Ladder is 18″ high; man is 2¾″ tall (45.7; 7 cm.) *Gift of Yvonne Forbath.*

Two pottery bells; left: red clay painted with tempera colors, made at Ocotlán; right: angel, black clay burnished before firing, made at San Bartólo Coyotepec. Height: 4¾" and 4" (12.1 cm. and 10.2 cm.)

Two "caricature" fruits with figures emerging—pottery painted in tempera colors and varnished. Made by Carlos and Margarito Panduras at Tlaquepaque, Jalisco. The two pieces shown represent a Cardinal and a Vera Cruz farmer in typical native dress; other caricatures in these surrealistic little pieces include clowns and policemen. Height 1¾" (4.4 cm.)

Turtle whistle, black burnished pottery, fired once; made at San Bartólo Coyotepec, Oaxaca. 4½" × 3" (11.4 × 7.6 cm.)

Two pottery figures, man and woman; red clay painted with tempera colors in blue, white and black. Made at Ocotlán, Oaxaca. Man, height 3¾″ (9.5 cm.)

Dog, mold-cast black burnished pottery.
2¾ × 2⅜″ (7 × 6 cm.)

Scorpion woven of palm leaf strips, dyed green. Length 2⅞″ (7.3 cm.)

Cart of red devils pulled by a team of orange oxen; carved and painted wood; a rather outlandish but witty creation of Manuel Jiménez of Arrasola, Oaxaca and requiring no complicated interpretation. Height of oxen 4¼″, cart 6½″ (10.8 and 16.5 cm.) *From the collection of Jean and Russell Ames.*

Four small, flat creatures: turtle, mouse, devil and burro woven or plaited out of wheat straw—*panicua*—for decorations or playthings. Height 3″ to 4″ (7.6 to 10:2 cm.)

Dog, carved and painted copal wood colored with yellow aniline dye and india ink. The legs are carved in one piece with the body, making a strangely primitive and stiff little animal. Length 7¾", height 7½" (19.7 × 19.1 cm.)

Turtle-rattle, mold-made clay with seeds or beads inside to make a rattle, painted with tempera colors: white, red and green. One of the oldest known toys in Mexico, and still made at Jamiltepec, Oaxaca. 4¼" × 2½" (10.8 × 6.4 cm.)

Fanciful Cat-tiger, carved and painted copal wood; by
Jiménez: Yellow and black with a red mouth. Height 4½″,
length 8½″ (11.4 × 21.6 cm.) *From the collection of Jean and
Russell Ames.*

Lion, carved and painted copal wood by Jiménez; yellow
body with black stripes, orange mane; legs and tail attached
with nails. Height 6″, length 14½″ (15.2 × 36.8 cm.) *From the
collection of Jean and Russell Ames.*

Kangaroo, carved and painted copal wood, yellow and black with a magenta baby painted in the pocket (front view); made by Manuel Jiménez of Arrasola, Oaxaca. Height 10″ (25.4 cm.) *From the collection of Jean and Russell Ames.*

Kangaroo, side view.

Group of Jiménez' animals, standing menacingly outside his farm house at Arrasola, Oaxaca.

Pottery hen (duck?) bank standing on three legs; buff clay, fired and decorated with reddish brown and brown colors. Made at San Agustín de las Flores, Guerrero. Height 4¼″, length 4″ (10.8 × 10.2 cm.) *From the collection of Jean and Russell Ames.*

Pottery horse and rider; red clay, fired and decorated with white tempera. Made at Ocotlán, Oaxaca. Height 6″, length 5″ (15.2 × 12.7 cm.) *From the collection of Jean and Russell Ames.*

Pottery lion with a long pompadour, fired buff clay painted in red and brown. Made at Ameyaltepec, Guerrero. Height 4″ (10.2 cm.) *From the collection of Jean and Russell Ames.*

Pottery animal with baby on its back; red clay, burnished and fired. Made at Acatlán, Oaxaca. Height 7″, length 5½″ (17.8 × 14 cm.) *From the collection of Jean and Russell Ames.*

Pottery Church by Candelario Medrano with cross on top—painted in tempera colors: green, pink, yellow and black, with small figures lounging about in a most undignified fashion. Height about 18″ (45.7 cm.) Photographed at BANFOCO, Mexico City.

Pottery Castle by Candelario Medrano, of weird design and occupied by nightmarish creatures: dragons, birds, dogs, a whale (?) and a few people; painted with tempera colors: red, yellow, blue, black and white. Height about 18″ (45.7 cm.) Photographed at BANFOCO, Mexico City.

Small pottery figures called *"Tanguyus"*—a Zapotec Indian word that means "Mistresses of the Land." The figures are painted in tempera colors and are often given as a group for semi-serious wedding and engagement gifts—sometimes a New Years gift. They are purposely made with a rather silly look, and carelessly painted—at Tehuantepec and Oaxaca City, as well as at other pottery centers. Heights of the (always female) figures range from 3″ to 5½″ (7.6 to 14 cm.)

48

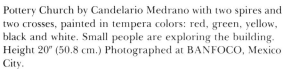

Pottery Church by Candelario Medrano with two spires and two crosses, painted in tempera colors: red, green, yellow, black and white. Small people are exploring the building. Height 20″ (50.8 cm.) Photographed at BANFOCO, Mexico City.

Pottery *alebrije,* fantastic animal figure and whistle, buff clay painted with white and brown tempera stripes. Made in Ocumicho, Michoacán. Height 6½″ (16.5 cm.)

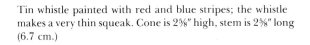

Tin whistle painted with red and blue stripes; the whistle makes a very thin squeak. Cone is 2⅝″ high, stem is 2⅝″ long (6.7 cm.)

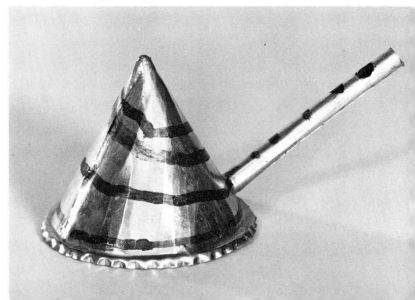

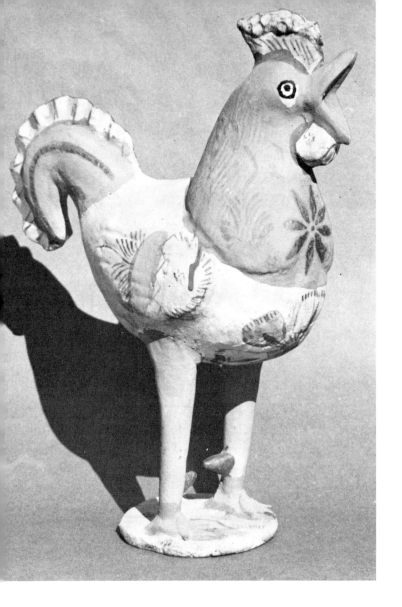

Pottery rooster painted in tempera colors: white, pink, yellow and dark blue. Made at Metepec, State of Mexico. Height 12″, length 9½″ (30.5 × 24.1 cm.) *From the collection of Jean and Russell Ames.*

Pottery figure with horns and flower-decorated pots, buff unglazed clay; marked inside with the initials of Teodora Blanco, but may possibly be the work of one of her many imitators, since the technique is not up to her standards. Made in Santa María Atzompa, Oaxaca. Height 6″ (15.2 cm.)

50

Pottery "Embroidered Doll" decorated in the technique called *pastillaje,* or application of small bits of clay. Made by one of the most famous potters of Mexico, in her unique style—Teodora Blanco of Santa María Atzompa, Oaxaca. Height 8½″, width 4½″ (21.6 × 11.4 cm.) *From the collection of Jean and Russell Ames.*

Bird rattle, papier maché on a stick; the cheapest kind of mold-made toy with seeds or stones inside; painted blue, yellow, green, white and red; varnished. Height 4¾″, width 4″ (12.1 × 10.2 cm.)

Wooden puppet—Indian girl with movable arms operated by a cord; painted with tempera colors—brown, red and blue with black details. Height 5⅛″ (13 cm.)

Wooden puppet—Indian girl with arms extended.

Man in turned-up sombrero—one-string puppet. Head, hands and feet are made of clay, painted, the rest of the figure is the cloth costume with belt and scarf of foil paper. There are more than a dozen varieties of these little puppets, operated by a single wire fastened through the head; the figure dances up and down, and the arms and legs move because they are so limp. Height 7″ (17.8 cm.)

Pottery doll, primitively modeled and dressed; a copy of a very old doll made by the Lacondon Indians in the North sections of Chiapas, said to be the most primitive descendents of the Mayas. Height 6⅞″ (17.5 cm.)

Bull—papier maché, painted with tempera colors: pink body, gray, black and white. Length 8½″, height 5½″ (21.6 × 14 cm.)

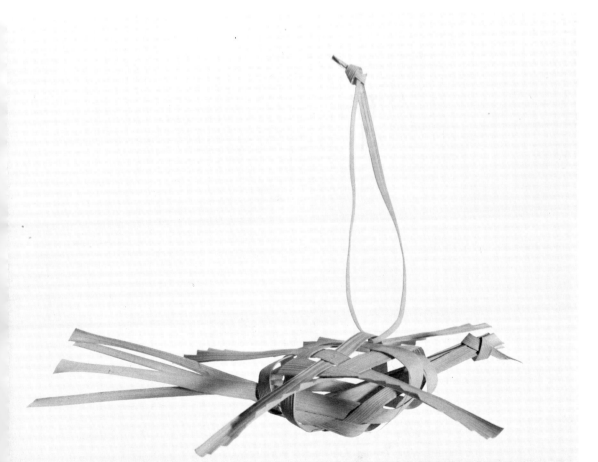

Palm leaf bird hanging ornament in natural golden color. Length 7″ (17.8 cm.)

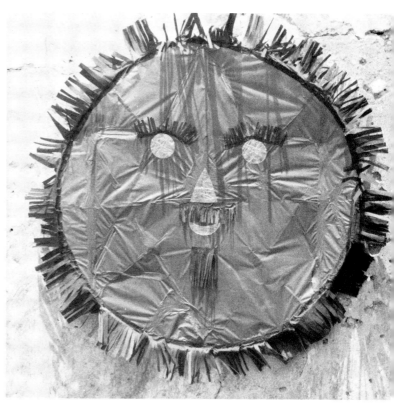

Kite—a star, made with a split reed frame, and orange tissue paper with green and pink ruffles strung on string. Made by Jaime Salvador of Oaxaca City. Width 34″ (86.4 cm.)

Kite—a sun, made with a split reed frame and pink and orange tissue paper, by Jaime Salvador of Oaxaca City. Diameter: 30″ (76.2 cm.)

Pottery candle holder painted in tempera colors; fancifully enlivened by figures of a child, a dog and a flying bird stuck on a wire; multicolored. Typical of the witty and amusing painted clay wares of Acatlán, Puebla. 7″ × 3″ × 5¾″ (17.8 × 7.6 × 14.6 cm.)

Pottery "Ark" painted with tempera colors, made by one of the most famous creators of original folk art pottery pieces in Mexico. The work of Candelario Medrano is described as "surrealistic," and his constructions with their small figures appearing to move in and out of doors and arches do indeed make these pieces lively and imaginative. Most of the modeling is done by hand; the Medrano workshop is in Santa Ana Acatlán, Jalisco, but the work is sold all over Mexico in fine shops. All Medrano pieces are painted in many bright colors; this ark flies the Mexican flag and is about 18″ tall (45.7 cm.) Photographed at BANFOCO, Mexico City.

Papier maché jointed dolls in the museum el Alhondiga at Guanajuato City.

56

II

MINIATURES

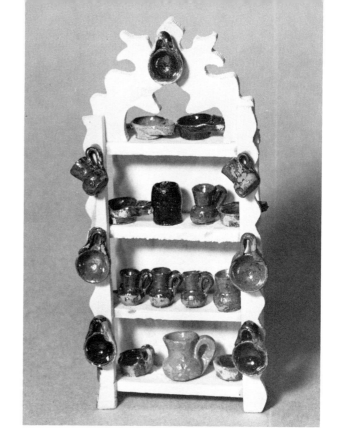

Miniature unpainted wooden shelf (*trastero*), a traditional piece of furniture in most Mexican kitchens. Holds tiny pots, some glazed green, some natural red with varnish. 3″ wide by 6¾″ high (7.6 × 17.1 cm.)

An almost unreasoning love for miniatures and a devotion to the sort of miniscule make-believe they embody are typical of many Mexicans. Artisans all over the country make a specialty of producing tiny objects which are to be found in quantity in markets and shops.

A permanent fixture in a corner pottery stall in the public market in Oaxaca is a post that is completely hung with—and concealed by—tiny green-glazed pots tied together by their handles, twelve to a string. They give the column the look of a tree trunk completely covered with a luxuriant tropical vine with small, shiny leaves. For a buyer, a circlet of a dozen pots is plucked off the display and sold for 8 pesos (formerly about 64 cents). The twelve pots on a string are of five or more different designs and the openings in the various shapes will barely accommodate the tip of one small finger. Year after year the *ollitas* are made by hand in the nearby village of Santa María Atzompa. They are shaped out of red clay, dried in the sun, coated with a dark green glaze, stacked in a kiln, fired, cooled and taken to market to be sold. When it is necessary to replenish the supply, the village potters (with the help of their children) make more pots and dump the finished pieces into a deep basket as if they were pouring out freshly-

harvested chick-peas ready to be sold. Miraculously, almost none of them are broken.

Practically every object to be seen in a Mexican home and scores of other things are reproduced in miniature—and they are made of every material known to the craftsmen of the country. Many adults collect miniature objects of all kinds—some are unbelievably delicate works of art made of blown glass, lacquer, inlaid shell or broomstraw, tin, copper and silver. The housewife arranges and guards her shelf of treasures while her children play with their own collections of simpler and less expensive thimble-sized tableware, tea sets, dolls, animals, furniture, swords, guns and toy soldiers. There are probably very few office desks and kitchen window sills in the Republic of Mexico that are not enlivened by at least one sort of diminutive ornament. (See color plates)

Some quirk of the fanciful imagination of Mexicans is surely stirred by small objects, the craze for which seems to be pervasive and everlasting. The liking for *pequeñitos* has a contagion about it, and many home-bound visitors take a box of trinkets with them when they leave the country, having acquired a taste for the national pastime—collecting Mexican miniatures.

Corn shuck "character" doll—little old lady wearing the triangular shoulder cape called a *quexquémetl*, with touches of red dye color representing embroidery. Height 3¾″ (9.5 cm.)

Miniature unpainted wooden cabinet with drawers and doors that open; on shelves: miniature pottery, copperware and figurines. 3″ wide by 6″ high (7.6 × 15.2 cm.)

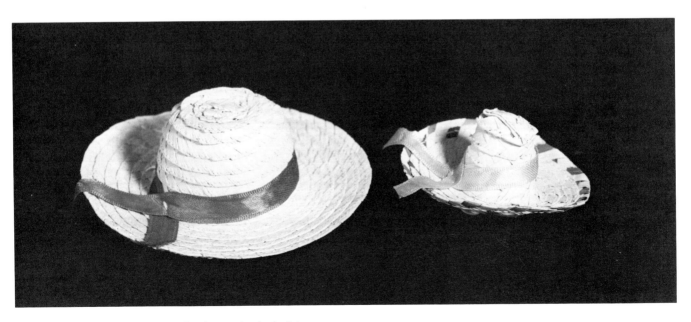

Two miniature doll hats made of natural palm leaf decorated with ribbons. Diameters 4¼″ and 3″ (10.8 and 7.6 cm.)

Miniature pottery tea set and tray; mold-cast clay, light brown glaze. Tray 2½″ × 4″, pitcher height 1½″ (6.4 × 10.2, 3.8 cm.)

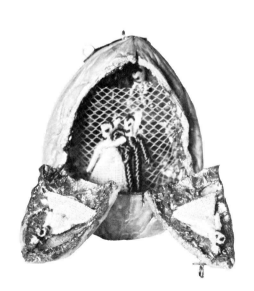

Wedding in a walnut; bride and groom in the center, and members of the wedding party in the two open doors; made at Guanajuato City. Height 1⅝″, figures ½″ (4.1, 1.3 cm.)

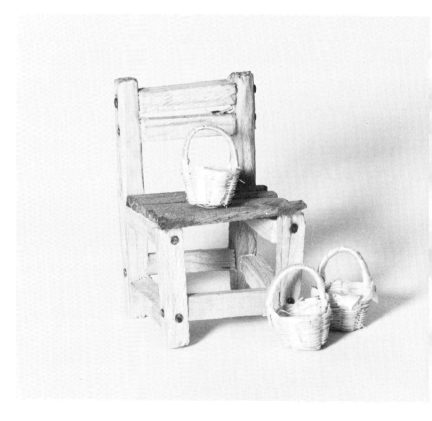

Little unpainted wood chair and three wheat straw baskets, natural color. Chair 1⅞″ × 3″; baskets height 1″ (4.8 × 7.6; 2.5 cm.)

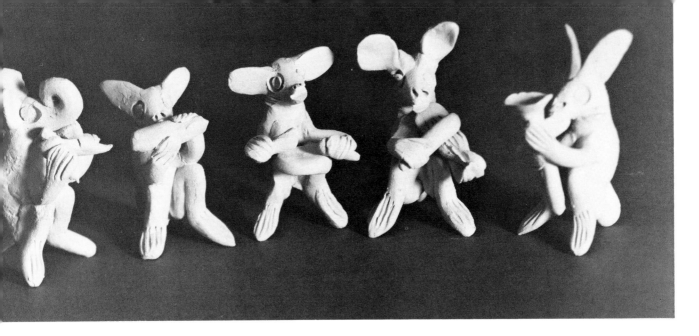

Animal musicians—these very small unglazed pottery figures are called *musiquitos,* are always made in sets of five, and the tiny fingers of the children of Santa María Atzompa, Oaxaca shape many of them. Height 1¾" (4.4 cm.)

Tea set, pottery of buff clay with blue-splashed decoration, mold-cast. Jug is 1½" high (3.8 cm.) *Gift of Mrs. Walter W. Frese.*

Miniature kitchen utensils—tin painted with red, white and blue enamel. Diameter of frying pan 2¾" (7 cm.)

Pony—milky pale green glass, hand-blown or "stretched";
made in Guadalajara, Jalisco. Height 1¾″ (4.4 cm.)

Mirrors with punched tin frames, painted with aniline colors
in red, green, magenta and yellow. Top, 2¼″ × 3¼″; bottom,
3¼″ diameter. (5.7 × 8.3 and 8.3 cm.)

Guitar made of unpainted wood, strung with
nylon "strings." Length 7½″, width 2½″
(19.1 × 6.4 cm.)

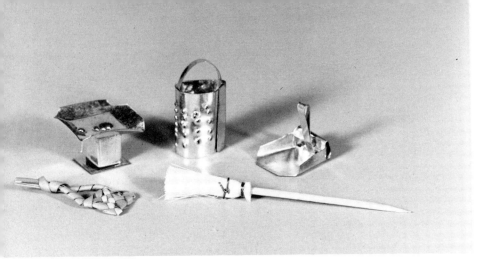

Household implements, left to right: charcoal brazier made
of tin, palm leaf fan for it, tin cheese grater and dustpan and
broom with a toothpick handle. Broom 3″ long (7.6 cm.)

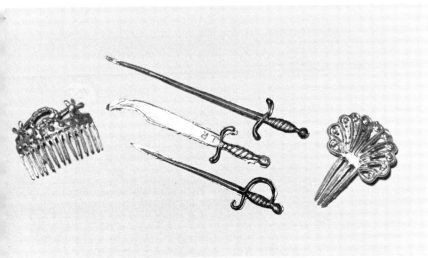

Five lead toys: two combs and three swords. Combs 1¼″
wide, longest sword 3⅜″ (3.2 and 8.6 cm.)

Shoe made of painted clay, purse and boots made of
leather. Boots are 1⅛″ high and the shoe is 1½″ long (2.9
and 3.8 cm.)

Four miniature household implements: rolling pin, basket, whisk broom and chocolate whisk—*molinillo* made of
wood, palm leaf and broomstraw. Basket ½″ tall, rolling
pin 1⅝″ long (1.3 and 4.1 cm.)

Plate made of *alfeñique* sugar paste, with tinted fruit; lead toys: tableware, iron and frying pan. Diameter of plate 1⅝″, knife 2³/₁₆″ long, pan ¾″ diameter. (4.1, 5.6 and 1.9 cm.)

Woman in kitchen in miniature room; painted clay and cardboard. Room: 1⁵/₁₆″ wide, 1¹/₁₆″ high, ½″ deep (3.3 × 2.7 × 1.3 cm.) A common pin is shown at the right.

Miniature head mask—carved wood animal painted in tempera colors in red, white and black. Made in Guadalajara, Jalisco. Height 4½″, width 3½″ (11.4 × 8.9 cm.) *Gift of Yvonne Forbath.*

Lead toys—pistol 2¾″ long (7 cm.) and an unlikely combination of horse, peacock and cow—the strip is 3⅞″ long (9.8 cm.)

Wedding in a walnut-shell turkey; two doors open to disclose the wedding couple. Made at Guanajuato City. (A rubber tail has been removed in order to photograph the object.) Height of figures ⅝″ (1.6 cm.)

Market figures, man and woman with their wares. Common pin in center. Painted clay. Height ⅞″ (2.2 cm.)

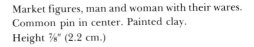

Corn shuck figures, painted. A common pin is shown at right. Height 1″ (2.5 cm.)

Toro—bull or ox—carved of copal wood and painted with aniline colors and India ink. This is a Manuel Jiménez masterpiece of stylization and animated simplicity. Length 10″, height 8¼″ (25.4 × 21 cm.)

Two rather elegant rag dolls;
cloth bodies stuffed with cotton
and carefully dressed in tribal
costumes; yarn hair and embroidered faces. Height 10½″ and 10″
(26.7 and 25.4 cm.)

Nopal cactus, native to all
the southern part of Mexico.

Little horse made of mold-pressed papier maché, gaily painted with tempera colors. Paper ears and a tail made of *ixtle* fiber have been added.
4½″ × 4¼″ (11.4 × 10.8 cm.)

Pottery animal gymnasts—from bottom to top: horse, pony, goat, dog and a flying bird. A joyful toy for all to behold. Length 6″, width 2¼″, height 14½″
(15.2 × 5.7 × 36.8 cm.)

Pig, carved wood painted with aniline colors; the legs and ears are attached with nails. This is certainly the head of a pig, but the shopowner insisted that the animal was a *dog*. Not visible in the photograph is the short, straight tail of a dog. Length 6″, height 3½″ (15.2 × 8.9 cm.)

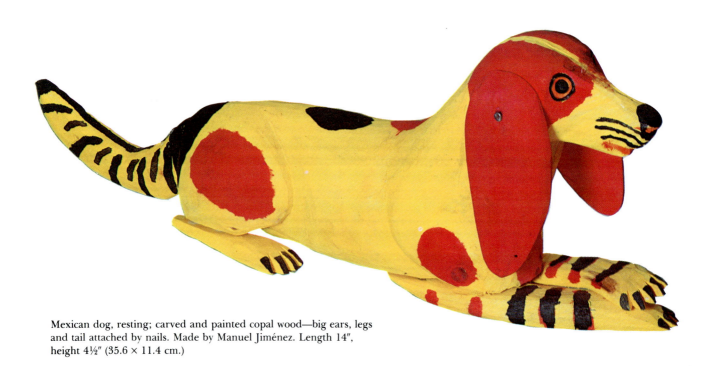

Mexican dog, resting; carved and painted copal wood—big ears, legs and tail attached by nails. Made by Manuel Jiménez. Length 14″, height 4½″ (35.6 × 11.4 cm.)

Lion (?) with a very small mane. Carved of copal wood and painted in aniline colors by Manuel Jiménez, Arrasola, Oaxaca. Length 13¾″, height 6¼″ (34.9 × 15.9 cm.)

Wood push-toy painted in aniline colors and topped with crêpe paper. When pushed, the merry-go-round turns, giving the ducks a ride. A primitively-made but cleverly-engineered toy. Height 10″ (25.4 cm.)

Chess pieces—the Queen and the bandit King of an oversized chess set. The basic forms are mold-pressed papier maché; details—hat, reed gun, braided hair and cord decorations added, and the figures are set on cardboard bases. The Queen's tunic and the King's cartridge belt are glued-on paper. See photograph on page 32 of the Knight chessman of the same set. Pieces painted in tempera colors, metallic gold and varnished. Made by Guadalupe Rodriguez, San Miguel de Allende, Guanajuato. Height 7″ (17.8 cm.)

Jiménez' red-spotted dog staring the world straight in the eye.

Horse (?): carved and painted wood. The strange proportions and quizzical look make this long-necked animal very funny; the carver would be sure to agree. Length 10½″, height 9⅜″ (26.7 × 23.8 cm.)

Pottery toy (sculpture?) painted in tempera colors. A whimsical group of performing dogs wearing caps, each with a bird perched (on a wire) on his hat. Made at Acatlán, Puebla. Length of base 9½″, width 3¼″, height 8″ (24.1 × 8.3 × 20.3 cm.)

The best-known doll in Mexico comes in many sizes and colors. She is mold-made of papier maché with movable arms and legs made separately and attached with cords. The lady looks like a glittery circus performer and comes with black, brown, orange or yellow hair, various-colored tights and bearing all the girls' names known in the country. Lola was made in Celaya, Guanajuato. Height 10″ (25.4 cm.)

III

RITES AND RITUAL OBJECTS

MYTHS AND WITCHCRAFT

Superstitions, myths and magic rituals were an important part of Indian cultures in Middle America long before the Spanish conquerors arrived in Mexico in the sixteenth century. The natives believed that the Universe is one great whole made up of all things, both living and inanimate, as well as the sun, moon, galaxies, water, land, wind, fire, thunder and lightning. Identical particles, they believed, unite to form birds, flowers, mountains and seas and man is made of the same stuff as the stars. The world is thus *one,* and everything in it has a soul of its own.

The Catholic religion that was introduced into Mexico by the Spanish had an omnipotent new God and an awe-inspiring liturgy. Soon there were towering churches built by the Spaniards, and they had gold and silver altars that were more impressive than anything the natives had ever seen. Smaller village churches were built all over the country—often on sites that had been sacred places of pagan worship.

But the new religion was accepted only in varying degrees by the Indians. Octavio Paz says their adherence to Catholicism was "passive." The natives already had strong tenets of their own and had great

faith in their gods and priests, and could not carry on their lives without the help of the *pueblo* medicine men, magicians or *shamans* of their tribes. Today, four hundred years later, ancient pagan beliefs and the rituals of Christendom have become inextricably woven together in Mexico so that they make a distinctive but erratic pattern. Small, abandoned Catholic churches in remote regions are used for magic-invoking ceremonies, while devout Christian pilgrims in cities may find their paths strewn with flower petals laid down in colorful Indian designs. The Aztec sun symbol is found on church façades among the figures of Christian saints and Spanish baroque scrolls. One belief held by most Mexicans is a combination of the two influences—it is that the physical disappearance of living things at death does not bring about the demise of the soul, but that the spirit remains alive and is actively present forever. This gives Mexicans a philosophy, it is said, which makes death an integral part of every life.

In the quiet fastness of a few mountain areas in Mexico there are several tribes that have remained untouched by Catholicism and still live by their centuries-old faith in supernatural powers and witchcraft. Notable among these are the Otomís of San Pablito in the *Sierra Madre Oriental* in the south central state of Puebla. In this rugged area there are still annual pilgimages to what is left of a village church built by the Spanish. But the ceremonies are pagan, not Christian, in spite of the colorful Spanish-style robes worn by the Indian participants. Other Indians who have not been influenced strongly by Christianity and who engage in ritual practices are the Huichols, the Coras and the Seris of the southern *Sierra Madre Occidental* along the west coast of Mexico near the juncture of the three states of Jalisco, Nayarit and Zacatecas. The Chimulas of San Cristóbal las Casas in the southern state of Chiapas are also still following their pre-Spanish beliefs.

Some isolated groups of mountain Indians are very self-sufficient, raise all their own food and live almost independently of the rest of the country. They carry on ancient rites to appease angry spirits, to bring death to their enemies, to assure love matches, to bring about good crops and to ensure the well-being of their families. Their rituals have been described by visitors who have made the rather arduous journey on foot or by horse or burro to visit the mountain *pueblos*.

The adornments used for pagan ceremonies and the magical objects and votive symbols that govern the lives of these natives are among the most unique traditional artifacts of present-day Mexico. Examples may be seen in museums, and some ritual objects made in less remote tribal communities are sent to the cities where they may be found in folk or art shops. (See color plates)

Bark Paper and the Otomí Indians of San Pablito

In ancient Mexico, paper made from tree bark was used to record history in codices that were written in hieroglyphic symbols and were enlivened by colored illustrations. The few of these books that remain are now preserved in museums and libraries and they tell us much about Mexico's early history. Bark paper was also used in pre-Hispanic times for decorating temples and for making ceremonial costumes.

The Otomí Indians in the mountain village of San Pablito, Puebla still carry on the making of bark paper by hand as the codices show it being done long ago. Today native women are pounding out the same kind of bark sheets, but until very recent years these

were reserved exclusively for use in local village ceremonies involving witchcraft and magic.

The Mexican Indian method of making sheets of paper from tree bark is done in a way very much like that used to make *tapa* cloth in the Pacific islands. The South Sea cloth is (or was) used for clothing and for making very large panels block printed in decorative patterns. It was not used primarily for ritual purposes. Both the Mexican and the South Sea papers are made from inner tree bark by slow hand methods and with only the simplest equipment.

In San Pablito two native trees supply most of the bark for paper—the mulberry tree for making sheets of a whitish color, and the wild fig tree for brown. A tree called *xalama* is sometimes used to make an almost black paper. In the *náhuatl* language the word for fig tree is *amatl*, but because the Spaniards found it difficult to pronounce "tl", they called it *amate*. Scientists still call it *amatl*, but it is now popularly known as amate-bark paper.

The Otomí Indians believe that the most propitious time for collecting bark is when there is a new moon; this will make the paper more effective for ritual use. Paper is an essential part of any magic-invoking procedures, and for a variety of primitive rites. Even the colors are important—the brown and white sheets are used for different purposes. Otomí men gather the bark, cutting it into sections about five feet long and a few inches wide, (1 m., 52.6 cm. × 76 cm.) pulling it off the trees in the spring, the season when stripping will do the least damage to growing trees. The pieces of bark are rolled and tied into bundles, then taken to the market to be bought

Otomí Indian woman boiling *amate* bark to prepare it for paper-making.

Otomí woman laying out wet strips of *amate* bark on wooden plaque, in preparation for pounding it out into a sheet of *amate* bark paper, San Pablito, Puebla.

by the women of the tribe, who do all the papermaking.

First the bark is soaked in a running stream to wash away the sap and to make it possible to separate the inner bark from the outer. The outer bark is discarded—only the inner bark is used. Then the bark strips are boiled in lime-water (in which corn has been soaked and cooked) in a large copper kettle over an open fire, and stirred with a sturdy pole. Washing and boiling are repeated until the fibers are soft, then the strips are taken out of the pot for a final rinse in the stream. The wet, flexible sections of bark are then pulled apart, twisted and cut into rope-like strips of shorter length; these are coiled and put into a large bowl of water so that they will stay soft and pliant.

Near the small outdoor working area are stacked many rough-hewn rectangular boards with smooth sides. These have been cut into the approximate sizes of the desired sheets of paper. Historically, the usual size was small—only about four by nine inches (10.2 × 22.9 cm.); larger sheets are made now also for commercial use. The woman sits on the ground with a board in front of her and lays out strips of damp bark fiber on it, first outlining the edges of the board, then adding more strips criss-crossing them in grid fashion. She then beats the fibers repeatedly with a flat, hand-sized stone about one and one-half inches thick which is grooved on the pounding surface. As she rhythmically pounds the strands of inner bark against the hard wood tablet, the fibers gradually spread and become felted together, finally forming a sheet of surprisingly uniform thickness. The sheet of paper fills the size and shape of the board. Then the tablet is set in the sun and left for the pounded amate-bark paper to dry. The sheets have slightly irregular edges and rounded corners, but they are never trimmed. When the material is completely dry the sheets can be peeled off the boards easily and the paper is finished. The paper has a slightly irregular surface but is pleasant to touch and is heavier than most commercial paper. Now it is the women's turn to fold and bundle up their sheets of paper and take them to the market to sell. The packets of paper—some brown and some white—will be bought by the local shaman—or medicine man—to use when he officiates at ceremonies, or by villagers who will give it to him to use when he performs magic rites on their behalf.

The principal use of amate paper is for making small paper "dolls" which are to be used by the witches, called *brujos* and *brujas* to represent spirits, devils, animals and human figures to impersonate gods or persons involved in the rituals. Medicine men also make use of candles, incense, herbs and live chickens in their ceremonial procedures. The decorative and skilfully-cut paper dolls shown in the illustrations are not used as playthings like paper dolls known in North America. These are not toys in any sense and they are made only by the designated men or women who are religious leaders, witch doctors and tribal magicians. The paper figures all have special meanings and functions.

In general, the dark brown paper is used for cut-outs that represent evil spirits, devils and vengeful gods, while the white paper dolls represent kindly spirits, beneficial gods and the persons on whose behalf the rite is conducted. There are other distinctive characteristics of the bark-paper figures. Dolls representing women have hair tufts on the head; dolls with shoes and those with heads of animals represent strangers (who wear shoes) and bad people, while figures with bare feet represent natives and good people. Brown paper dolls are always burned or destroyed after the rituals, but the good white dolls are saved to be carried as

Amate paper doll—a male animal representing an evil spirit with shoes. Figure 8″ tall (20.3 cm.) on brown *amate* paper sheet 8″ × 11¾″ (20.3 × 29.8 cm.)

Amate paper doll—a female figure that safeguards the bean crop. Figure 8″ tall (20.3 cm.) on brown *amate* paper sheet 8½″ × 12″ (21.6 × 30.5 cm.)

Amate paper doll—female figure with bare feet representing the spirit of the fruit tree. Figure 8¼″ tall (21 cm.) on brown *amate* paper sheet 7⅜″ × 11″ (18.7 × 27.9 cm.)

Amate paper figure representing a boar or peccary (?) embodying the spirit of evil people. Figure 9″ tall (22.9 cm.) on brown *amate* paper sheet 8″ × 11¾″ (20.3 × 29.8 cm.)

White *amate* paper doll—a female figure representing the spirit of a tree. Figure 7¼″ tall (18.4 cm.)

White *amata* paper figure of the two-headed bird representing the spirit of the mountains—*Den Xini.* This is one of the most powerful and beneficent figures, and is the guardian of the house. Figure 8¼″ tall (21 cm.)

White *amate* paper doll—a female figure representing the spirit of the tomato plant. Figure 8″ tall (20.3 cm.)

talismen for good luck, or to be hung in a doorway to guard the house and its occupants from evil spirits.

Since every Otomí Indian's life is surrounded by spirits that control his destiny, he must constantly court the favor of the gods and appease their anger when things go wrong. Therefore, the principal purpose of most ceremonies is to bring about the favorable disposition of the deities.

The services performed by the Otomí sorcerers are many and have no counterparts in Christian society. The native man or woman who officiates may at times act as a fortune teller, minister or priest, doctor, surgeon or psychiatrist and sometimes as a professional folk-singer, dancer and artist. He always has unquestioned power to invoke either good or evil.

An Otomí village may have several sorcerers, each serving a number of family groups. The most important magician is the *shaman,* and he, as well as the others, passes his skills on to a son, daughter or young relative who will follow the profession.

Each paper doll made and used by the magicians has a subtly different shape that is related to its purpose. Ancient paper figures may have been torn, but today's magician carries a pair of modern scissors with which he quickly and skilfully cuts the folded paper into the form he needs to use. All the sheets of paper are rectangular and are folded vertically, then cut and unfolded; all the figures are

therefore bisymmetrical. Some *brujos* use red, green or blue tissue paper (called China paper in Mexico) to make some of the dolls, but the natives believe bark paper to be more powerful. As soon as a doll has been cut out it acquires magic powers and the trimmings are destroyed so that they cannot be put to any evil use.

Many Otomí ceremonies are performed to bring rain and to make crops flourish; there is a doll to represent almost every fruit, vegetable and grain grown by the Indians. The Otomís depend on the medicine men to cure all illnesses and on the *brujos* to bring prosperity, good luck, and to guard their homes and families from harm. A native has complete faith in the magical powers of the little brown and white paper dolls that act out the drama of his life.

Travelers and collectors are also pleased with the small, ritual paper dolls and admire their exotic appearance and extraordinarily decorative forms. So, these are now made commercially and are sometimes to be found for sale.

A brief description of a few of the rites will give an idea of the nature and purpose of Indian ceremonies that make use of bark paper.

The *costumbre*

The most often-performed ceremony is complete in itself, or it may precede a more complicated rite. It is called the *costumbre,* or "custom", and it is a

Ritual act with cut-paper dolls on beds of *amate* paper. The *brujo* lights candles to start the ritual. San Pablito, Puebla.

sweeping or cleaning-out of all bad spirits that may be in the vicinity, or who might have entered into the body of a sick person. If the bad spirits are not removed first, they would interfere with any subsequent ritual. The sorcerer cuts out about eight or ten paper dolls, usually with animal heads, to represent bad spirits and he puts them in two rows on the ground, each lying on a specially-cut sheet of brown amate paper called a "bed." A candle is lighted at each corner of the space. The sorcerer squats down with a live chicken under one arm and begins to chant or pray in Otomí. After a time, he clips the neck of the chicken with scissors and sprinkles blood liberally over the dolls and bed. Then, still holding the chicken under his arm, he does a slow dance around the dolls, jumps back and forth over them and continues his sing-song chant. Finally, he picks up all the paper dolls and beds and wraps them around the dead chicken and runs about with the bundle so that it will absorb the bad spirits that still may be lingering nearby. Finally, he blows out the candles and runs off to fling the packet far down the mountainside, and the evil spirits go with it.

Ritual for the Spirit of the Field

To induce good crops, the magician begins by taking some earth from the four corners of a field and puts it into a new clay pot and adds offerings of chocolate, candles, sugar, other foods and two white paper dolls representing the Spirits of the Field. The pot is tightly covered and buried in the center of the field for two days. When the pot is dug up musicians begin to play and chant while the sorcerer carefully returns the earth to the corners of the field. Many of the Otomí ceremonial chants are accompanied by musicians playing traditional tunes on a primitive guitar and violin, repeating a few simple bars and phrases over and over again. There are three or four parts to this ceremony: the arrival, the *costumbre,* the rejoicing and the departure. Each part has its own music, words and actions. The field now cannot fail to produce a good crop.

The Spirit of the House

This is a long, elaborate ceremony of thanksgiving and finally of drinking and feasting. It is performed within two years after a house (usually a one-roomed hut) is built, to offer the house thanks for its protection to the owner and his family. Many white paper dolls are used to decorate a small altar, some are hung around the walls, and some are placed on an elaborate palm leaf star in the middle of the room. The cleaning ceremony is performed first, after which four young boys shoot arrows toward a sort of attic storage platform, then toward the roof of the hut. Musicians accompany the sorcerer and the four young archers as they chant and perform a complicated dance around the star. Incense is burned, and the whole house is decorated with flowers. Thus thanked, the house is the scene of a neighborly fiesta.

The Costumbre of the Well

The well is the center of village life and is vital to the people. If it is suspected that illness has come from drinking the water, it is then believed that an evil spirit has entered the spring that feeds the well. The sorcerer performs the *costumbre* at the spring. When the evil spirits have been swept away, offerings of eggs and candles and a paper doll representing the Spirit of the Well are buried. Then burning of incense and songs and dances by the magician accompany the decorating of the well with dolls representing the Guardian, the Door and the Flower of Heaven. These will purify the water, and all will be safe.

...has been abandoned by her man,
...n the sorcerer to bring back her
...cuts out two dolls, one represents
...other the woman; the man's arms
...nd the woman. The dolls are held in
...he incense, the sorcerer blows into their
...magical chants and motions are per-
...e dolls are then given to the woman with
...ed instructions as to what she must do. She
...ed" the dolls when she eats, she must take
...o bed with her, and she must burn a candle
...day. If she follows all the instructions closely,
...man will return.

Affairs of Hate

The magician is sometimes asked to intervene in personal troubles between two villagers. If a man wants revenge for a wrongdoing, a doll is made of brown paper to represent his antagonist and a cactus thorn is stuck into its heart. The doll is secretly buried near the enemy's house where it will put a curse on him and cause pain and sickness.

This description of bark paper ceremonies may give a picture of Otomí life that seems to be made up principally of problems and dilemmas. This is not so. The Indians are generally contented and hard-working and although they are poor in material possessions, they have their happy moments. Otomí women are known as skilled weavers and both women and little girls wear the short shoulder-cape called a *quechquémetl* which is sometimes left plain and sometimes embroidered. The weavers use both wool and cotton for their handsome fabrics.

The Otomís and some other mountain tribes are not hospitable to strangers, whom they call *mestizos* or *ladinos* generally meaning citified people. The Indians do not welcome visitors and seldom allow them to witness their rites and acts of *brujería* or witchcraft.

Many Otomís live in less isolated areas than those of San Pablito. These other people also practice witchcraft and pagan rituals, but they have much more contact with other Mexicans. On occasion, the Otomís perform some spectacular tribal dances, and young village dancers are proud of their talents and do not mind having an audience for their perform-ances. The Indians of Pahuatlán, Hidalgo are one of several groups that make a specialty of the *Juego de Volador,* or the Flying Pole Dance, which is not really a dance, but rather one of the most breath-taking acrobatic spectacles of Mexico. The Otomís also perform a ceremonial dance called the *Acatlaxqui,* or

Dance of the Reed Throwers. This colorfully cos-tumed dance starts as a stately folkloric dance, but is climaxed by the "throwing out" of decorated reed arches, the ringing of church bells and a noisy burst of fireworks as great rockets light up the night.

The Huichols of Jalisco, Nayarit and Zacateca

The Huichols are mountain people, descen-dants of the Aztecs who fled into the moun-tains of the southern *Sierra Madre Occidental* when news reached them of the final success of the Spanish invasion in 1521. It was not until two hundred years later that Spanish missionaries were able to reach the almost inaccessible Huichol *pueblos*; and even after a few Catholic churches were built, the natives con-tinued to worship their own gods and have stead-fastly clung to their ancient pagan beliefs. Their name originally meant *healers,* and today about one fourth of the men are said to be shamans or sorcerers. A few saints and saints' days have been incorporated into Huichol celebrations, but the people have never been converted to the Christian faith and have almost never intermarried with the Spanish. The Huichols therefore remain of essentially pure Aztec blood in a country where most traditions and much of the heritage is now Spanish. They are generally believed to have retained more pre-Hispanic customs and rituals than any other Indian tribe of Mexico.

The extremely rugged mountains of western Mexico have indeed afforded the Huichols the pro-tection and isolation they sought in the 16th century. The precipitous ravines have never been bridged and there is no way to cross turbulent rivers during the long rainy season to reach the mesas and valleys where scattered *pueblos* are located. In the best of seasons, the journey to Huichol land is a demanding and strenuous undertaking for visitors.

The members of this unique tribe are said to number about 9,000, who dwell in five independent communities with five "capitol" *pueblos* that are both religious sites and seats of government. Each group has its own autonomous officers—usually the heads of the principal families. Every community guards its own borders, and has distincitive small differences in dress, customs and the Indian language. Members of a group may live as far as a five days' trip away from other villages of the same group. Surprisingly, the intelligent Huichols have not sought complete isola-tion from the rest of modern Mexico, and certain young men are taught the Spanish language with the

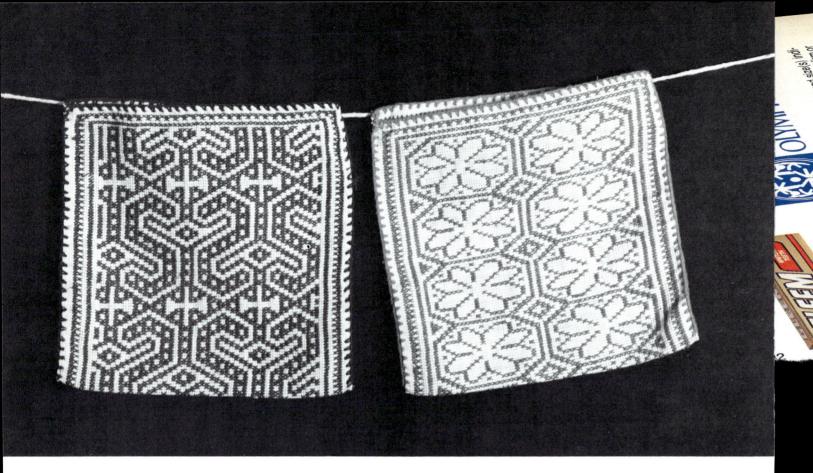

Two Huichol Indian waist-bags worn by men; plainly woven of cotton, design in cross-stitch in traditional patterns, one in red, the other in blue. 6½″ square (16.5 cm.)

expectation that they carry on communications with the other peoples of their country. The Huichols are not wary of visitors, and the handsome Huichol ritual objects and artifacts that are still made in designs of hundreds of years ago find their way to city markets where they are prized by buyers with an eye for color and design. (See color plates)

The Deities

The Huichol has many gods and his beliefs are in many ways similar to those of the Otomís. He believes that the world is controlled by the sun and rain gods of the upper world and by the earth, water and fire gods of the lower world. The deities are in a constant state of displeasure with man, but the *shamans* know all the secrets of controlling godly ire and the people have only to follow the prescribed rituals and carry the proper amulets to enjoy the benevolence of their changeable deities. A Huichol's thoughts are almost completely occupied with his magic world, and everyone else in his community is bound to him by identical beliefs. The people know that when their gods are pleased by offerings and festivals, the omnipotent spirits will watch over and protect them

all. Frances Toor says: "In the more primitive groups, because of a greater number of gods to feast, the ceremonies and festivals in their honor sometimes require about one half of a man's time."

Dress

The Huichols appear to have an innate sense of color and design; their dress and ritual objects are distinctive. Both men and women wear necklaces of fine blue and white beads, and the women wear bracelets and earrings to match. Both also paint designs on their faces and these have significance when the wearers are participating in certain rituals. Huichol men have the most colorful everyday dress of all the Mexican Indians. Over the conventional white cotton blouse and pants, the men wear a string of small, handwoven bags tied around their waists, all of which have meaning as good luck talismens. Larger bags are worn over each shoulder—these serve as the Huichol man's pockets. During rituals the men wear flat, wide-brimmed ceremonial hats decorated with feathers, fur and ribbons and with small stone or metal discs hanging from the edge of the brim. Shamans of the tribe wear bright handwoven capes, feathers, hair bands and bracelets when performing rituals. Women's dress is more conventional and much less colorful.

72

Sites of Worship

The most important religious sites of the Huichols are the sacred caves in which the gods are believed to have been born and where they supposedly still live. The rough caves are in remote, inaccessible locations and are occupied by a primitively-built altar and sometimes by small stone god-figures. Countless votive offerings are carried long distances by pilgrims who travel difficult miles on foot to deposit their gifts at the shrine of a particular god.

Each of the five principal *pueblos* has a ceremonial plaza surrounded by a circle of structures—a large one housing the main altar, and smaller huts that serve as shrines for various parts of the rituals. All the men and women in the village take part in the seasonal, days-long ceremonies and each person has official duties to perform. Eating is a climactic part of the more important rites at which a sacrificial bull or ox is cooked and consumed at a final village feast.

Huichol Indian shaman holding a sacred stick called a *muwiéri*; through it he can talk to deities, pray for their blessings and pray for rain. The stick, or wand is wrapped with colored yarns, and has feathers at the end. In the background are seen two of the small shrines that form part of the ceremonial circle of buildings used during ceremonies.

Symbols

Huichol symbols are unlike those of any other Mexican tribes, and in all their rites the Huichols honor their tribal gods, many of whom are represented by animals. The sun god is represented by the deer which always runs from east to west and is a benevolent god. The hawk and eagle are associated with the sky and are also good gods; their feathers are used in many ways to symbolize flight and power. The moon is symbolized by the rabbit—the creature that is seen in the moon by the Huichols. The snake is crooked like lightning and so represents a bad god. All Huichol votive objects using animals as designs have religious significance. The *nearíkas*, or wooden tablets with yarn designs applied to a beeswax base, and the *chaquiras*, or bead-decorated gourd bowls all bear beautiful and meaningful designs. Rituals frequently include the use of candles, incense, flowers and fruit—all offered to please the gods.

Huichol Indian god figure, painted pottery. Small stone or ceramic figures are set up on primitive altars in the sacred caves in secluded mountain areas. Scores of offerings are left around the god figure: stone prayer discs, yarn *nearíkas*, deer horns, prayer arrows, bead-decorated gourd *chaquiras* and corn. Height 7″ (17.8 cm.).

73

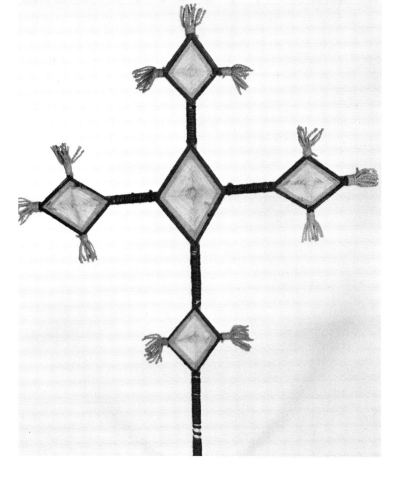

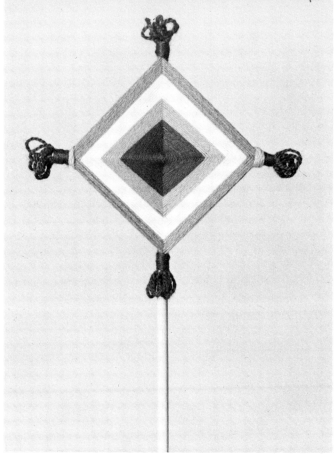

Huichol Indian votive plaque or *nearíka* made of wool yarn fixed in a coating of beeswax on a wood tablet. The designs of these *tablillos* have deeply religious significance in the Huichol religion; man and serpents appear often as a subject. Colors: deep red background with pink, yellow, orange and white wool. 11⅝″ square (29.5 cm.)

Huichol Indian "Eye of God"—*ojo de dios*—a protective ritual object made of wool yarn wound on two crossed sticks; colors: blue, red, green and white. 3¾″ square (9.5 cm.)

The *ojo de dios* (Eye of God) is a very old Indian symbol and has been known in many civilizations—possibly as early as 300 B. C. in Peru; it is said that it originally represented the four directions, North, South, East and West. This is a design formed by wrapping colorfully-dyed yarns around two crossed sticks to form a square with a center that somewhat resembles an eye. Essentially it invokes the favorable glance of the gods. The Huichols regard it as a special talisman for the welfare of children, and it is also associated with food, rain and sun. For the ceremony called the Dedication of the Children to the Sun, the young, bright-eyed Indians are literally covered with yellow flowers, bright feathers and God's Eyes to invoke the blessings and protection of the gods.

Other votive objects presented to the gods at Huichol altars are feather-trimmed prayer arrows, stone prayer discs, yarn prayer discs, deer horns as well as the *ojos de dios*. Food is also offered, such as ears of fresh corn, tortillas, tamales and corn cakes baked in the shapes of animals.

Ojo de dios, Huichol Indian votive symbol made with five "eyes of God"; yarn colors: red, blue, orange and yellow. Width 16″, height 20¾″ (40.6 × 52.7 cm.)

Music

The Huichols are fond of music, but all of it is of a religious nature. Their ceremonies are long, deeply serious and as carefully planned as an opera. Rituals often include native music played on a primitive violin and guitar—instruments that were introduced into Mexico by the Spanish. Chants and songs are part of the rites for which the best singers of the community are trained.

The Twentieth Century Huichol

More and more Indian youths are beginning to leave their native tribe to do seasonal work in the valley farms, and some of the boys do not return. A few airstrips have now been built on the Huichol mesas, and modern farm machinery is being introduced, so the distinctive group stands in danger of losing its primitive individuality to mechanization.

Huichol Indian playing a violin to provide ceremonial music—the instrument is held in the traditional Mexican Indian way.

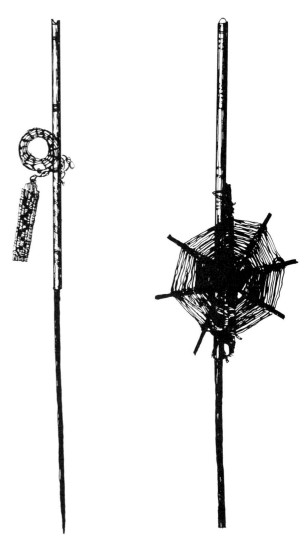

Huichol Indian Prayer Arrow made to be stuck in the ground at an altar in a sacred cave. The woven panel bears a votive symbol, and tied to the arrow are tail and wing feathers of the eagle and hawk—both considered to be sacred. The attached miniature rabbit snares have mystical powers. Height about 25″ (63.5 cm.).

Two Huichol Indian Prayer Arrows made to be used as offerings at the altar of a god. Both are adorned with yarn "prayer discs"; the smaller one also bears a woven magical symbol. Height about 25″ (63.5 cm.).

The Coras

The Cora Indians dwelling in the Sierra of Nayarit also still devoutly worship their pagan gods, and Frances Toor in her book describes the Coras thus:

"In the remote villages where there are few outsiders, the natives do their best to get rid of them; in a few places strangers have been driven out. These primitive groups usually have separate temples for their pagan and Christian rituals. When it happens, as among the Coras of Jesús María, Nayarit and elsewhere, that the natives use the same church as the *ladinos*, the two groups avoid going to worship at the same time. In Tanajapa, Chiapas, where there are numerous *ladino* families living permanently in the village to which the natives come only on market days or for fiestas and official business, the saints of the *ladinos* are on one side of the church dressed in expensive Spanish-style robes, while the 'saints' of the Indians are on the other side, resembling the natives in dress and looks."*

The Coras, like others, do recognize several Christian saints and these are especially honored if it happens that a church or village bears a saint's name. In San Juan Carapán, Nayarit, June 24 is celebrated as *el día de San Juan,* or the Day of Saint John the Baptist. One part of the fiesta is community bathing in the streams, and even the statue of San Juan is bathed!

Toor also says,

"Music plays an important part in the lives of the Coras, but it is chiefly religious. They have special chants for their pagan ceremonies and other secular songs in their own Indian language. Practically all the men know how to make reed flutes and their other instruments are drums, violins, triangles, rattles with metal discs and the *mitote.* The latter is a curious wooden instrument played only by medicine men. It is a long, curved slender wooden bow with a thin rope stretched between the two ends. The rope is 'played' with two sticks, and a gourd resting on the ground acts as a sounding board while two men adjust the bow with their feet."

The Coras live the same sort of life as the Huichols, but are poorer and prefer to remain much more remote from society. The men's dress includes strings of small, handwoven bags, but the Coras' appearance is comparatively drab, notwithstanding this sartorial touch.

*Toor, page 97.

Seri Indian woman with face painting; Kino Bay, Sonora.

The Seris

This tribe that pursues pagan beliefs lives mainly in the state of Sonora, and its members are called the most musical of all the primitive Indian groups in Mexico. The medicine men are called *song-makers* and they compose and sing chants and songs for all their rituals. Seri music, to the ears of outsiders, sounds the most melodic of all Mexican pagan ritual music.

Seri women are different in stature and appearance from other Indian women. They are often tall and slender with long, handsome faces, and they dress in gracefully simple long, two-piece cotton dresses in bright colors. The women's principal ornament is face-painting which they believe enhances their looks and it also serves to indicate their marital status. Young girls wear a small black semitransparent "mask" painting and the married women paint their faces in a green design.

Summary

The Indian tribes mentioned above and a few others such as the Chimulas of Chiapas have continued for centuries to pursue their pagan beliefs and they revere their all-powerful gods as a part of life and nature. The more isolated natives know almost nothing of the rest of the world, and they teach each new generation of Indian children the rites that are important to their way of living. The people are mostly serene and contented and some are fiercely proud of their tribal ways. In the remote regions it is possible that change simply never will occur as long as the people choose to maintain themselves independently.

Mexican Indian rituals are decidedly compelling, even to *ladinos* who cannot feel the deep emotional fervor that inspired them and has kept the ceremonies alive for so long.

Present-day visitors to rural Mexico will find many areas where the native Indians pursue a simple life much like that of natives of several hundred years ago. Even a comparatively large and busy southern Mexico city like Oaxaca with two fine museums and many good hotels is ringed by Zapotecan Indian *pueblos* where the Indian language is still used, farming and handcrafts are important pursuits and where life goes on at the unchanged pace of long ago. Customs may differ slightly in different tribes and from village to village, but one can still find a great variety of folk crafts and many of these are influenced by the beliefs and symbols of ancient Mexico.

MASKS OF THE STATE OF OAXACA

In the Regional Museum adjoining the beautiful Santo Domingo church in Oaxaca City there is an impressive collection of ritual masks from various Indian villages in the area. The masks are primitively carved of dark wood, all are very heavy and they range in height from 12 to 18 inches (30 to 45.2 cm.). Since many villages in central Oaxaca are still populated by Zapotecan Indians, some of the masks may be presumed to belong to their rituals. The date of the use of the masks is evidently uncertain, as the museum text says:

"Many years ago, in mountain areas that were inaccessible, before the arrival of teachers and missionaries people depended upon their own pagan gods for guidance, and masks were used as symbols of the gods and elements, for ceremonies and celebrations. Between ceremonies, the masks were kept in stone huts on the rocky plateaus. Masks were also used in fiestas as a part of the activities of the dancers, and of prayers and recitations."*

*Author's translation.

Mask, carved wood, representing the *Judge*. The mask was worn by the village judge who rode a burro, wearing a crown of acacia flowers, and performed marriages wearing this symbol of his office. From Santa María Estetla, Etla, Oaxaca.

Mask, primitively carved of dark wood, representing the *God of planting time* (sowing) in the fields. He is the protector of animals, the ill, and of engaged couples. From San Isidro Yucuntindo, Nochixtlan, Oaxaca.

Mask of the *Launderer of Wool*—an important official who was in charge of washing wool for weaving. From Santa María Estetla, Etla, Oaxaca.

Mask of the *God of the Fireworks Makers* who was in charge of supplying the powder for making *castillos* for fiestas. From Sola de Vega, Oaxaca.

Mask of the *God of the Skulls*. On November 2 the mask was carried from house to house in search of souls, accompanied by four ceremonial dancers, who intoned prayers and recitations. From Sola de Vega, Oaxaca.

IV

THE TOYMAKER AND
ARTISAN AT WORK

A BRIEF ENCYCLOPEDIA OF
MEXICAN METHODS, MATERIALS AND MAGIC

ANYONE WHO has ever stood watching a weaver working at his loom, or a potter shaping his clay knows that hand-made objects have a dual interest. The appearance of a finished object and the way it fulfills its purpose (even if that is simply to be decorative) are of principal interest. But the way a

A

Abalone Shell

This lustrous, irridescent shell from the sea is used for making inlaid designs in wood and pottery objects—mostly in wood miniatures. Tiny violins, guitars and other stringed instruments no longer than two and one-half inches (6.4 cm.) are made of fine-grained brown wood and are strung up with fine nylon cord secured by carved tuning pegs the size of

thing is made and the material that goes into it are factors with their own fascination, and knowledge of these adds a second dimension to an observer's appreciation of a piece when it is finally finished as the artist intended it to be.

a pin. The instruments are decorated with abalone cut-out borders and designs of flowers, leaves, stems and birds inlaid on both the front and back. The pieces of shell are cut by hand, smoothed, polished and set into a special black lacquer that has been applied to the wood. Then the dried, finished pieces are buffed until they are as smooth and shiny as glass. Each musical instrument comes in a small, felt-lined wooden box with a sliding lid.

Abalone is also sometimes used as an inlaid decoration on miniature mirror frames, small boxes, domino sets and pieces of unglazed black pottery.

Guitar carved of wood, trimmed with abalone shell inlay; the nylon strings are attached to pegs that really turn. Guitar is 2¼" long (5.7 cm.) and the box in which it comes is 1½" × 2¾" (3.2 × 7 cm.)

Back of the miniature guitar, inlaid with a shell design of remarkable detail.

This work is done largely in Valle de Mezquital and Ixmiquilpan, Hidalgo. The pieces are works of art, and the collector of Mexican miniatures feels that they are far too precious to be used as toys by small children.

Amate Bark Paper

This paper is made by Otomí Indians for use in their rituals, as described in Chapter III, but in recent years, brown amate paper has begun to be produced for another purpose, and is made in sheets as large as 18 by 25 inches (46 × 63.5 cm.). These are used by artists, especially in the state of Guerrero, to make brightly-colored tempera paintings in a style similar to that of their pottery, which is decorated with flowers, scrolls and fanciful animals and birds. The amate bark paintings may be bought in native markets or in city shops all over Mexico.

Amate bark painting done with tempera colors: red, white, blue, green, orange and black on brown paper. 9" × 12¼" (22.9 × 31.1 cm.)

Painting on *amate* bark—tempera colors on brown paper—white, green and black. 12″ × 8″ (30.5 × 20.3 cm.)

Aniline Colors

These strong dyes, obtainable in powdered form from a chemist's shop are synthetic, organic colors compounded from nitrobenzene, and have been in use as colorants since their discovery in 1856. Because *añilinos* are used to give many toys and ornaments the characteristic red, orange, yellow and magenta colors that are so typically Mexican—and are also used for the much less typical green and blue—we consider them to be important materials of the popular arts. The powders are simply mixed with alcohol and applied with a brush to paint both wooden and tin toys and decorations to give them a lively, clear transparent color. All the painted wooden animals and figures, the ferris wheel and other wooden toys, and the tin ornaments and toys shown in the photographs in this book (except a few that are enameled) are painted with aniline colors. In time the dyes will fade somewhat, and they also will rub off wood that is handled; they are more permanent on tin. But, in the meantime, they are bright and showy—and are happily very inexpensive for the artisans who use them.

Tin sun face, hand-embossed and soldered, painted orange and gold. Made by Aarón Velasco Pachico, Oaxaca City. Diameter 5¾″ (14.6 cm.)

Wood guitar decorated with applied, dyed broomstraw in many colors on both front and back. Length 4⅝″ (11.7 cm.)

B

Beads

Beads of many kinds are worn by Mexican Indians—and are a tribal identification; for instance, the Huichol Indians of the Sierra Madre Occidental mountains wear tiny blue and white beads in multiple strands. One distinctive use of beads in handcrafts is as applied decoration to the ceremonial gourd bowls of the Huichols. Round sections of dried gourds about five to seven inches (12.7 to 17.8 cm.) in diameter are coated inside with an even layer of sun-softened beeswax. Then the bright glass beads of tiny size (brought into Mexico by European traders) are carefully applied one by one to the wax and pressed into it to make solidly beaded designs of animals, people and other traditional, symbolic patterns that are important to the Huichol religion. The finished, very decorative votive bowls are called *chaquira*—the Spanish word for beads. The *chaquira* are among the most important offerings left on the altars of the Huichol gods—they are significant in themselves and are not used as containers. These unique bowls may be seen in ethnic displays in the anthropological museums of Mexico and elsewhere, and occasionally a few are found in government-sponsored popular arts shops. (See color plate)

Mexican Indians also make small woven or needle-worked beaded bags, bracelets and belts similar to those made by North American Indians. The children of San Bartólo Coyotepec, Oaxaca make black unglazed pottery beads that are eagerly purchased by visitors.

Boar Bristles

One of the most universally traditional masks in Mexico is that worn in the Dance of the Tigers. It is a fierce-looking face that has its origin in the stylized head of the pre-Hispanic sacred jaguar. The mask, whether large enough to be worn, or small to be used only as a decoration, is carved out of wood and is always characterized by large eyes, a red tongue, and a ring of bristling whiskers made from boar bristles. (See color plate) Many masks are produced in Olinalá, Guerrero, and the best of them are made by the traditional *rayada* (incised) lacquer technique; many of the masks are painted with glossy enamels.

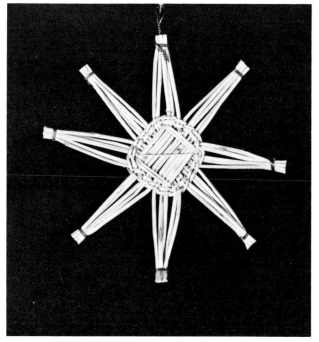

Broomstraw star ornament. Diameter 2¾″ (7 cm.)

Broomstraw

This lowly material is the wiry end-branches of a plant called broomcorn, or in Mexico, *popote*. Native artisans, with their gift for finding natural and inexpensive materials for making craft objects, have used their ingenuity and imagination to make some surprisingly decorative pieces from this usually entirely utilitarian straw.

The broomstraw star is woven together and fastened near the center with a few flexible strands of thin straw (possibly some type of grass) and the heavier broomstraws that form the points of the star are carefully matched in weight and length; the ends are secured with fine copper wire. The airy, little hanging ornament is cleverly and skilfully made.

The miniature guitar is 4⅝ inches long (11.7 cm.), carefully carved of wood and strung with six pieces of fine nylon cord, each wound onto its own tiny peg. The entire surface of the guitar except the neck is covered with designs of broomstraw dyed in five colors, cut and applied to the wood with glue. The front is decorated with an abstract pattern, and the back has a Mexican street scene in sunset colors. This is a painstaking work of folk art made for collectors of miniatures, not for children to use as a plaything.

83

Red clay pottery armadillo with two weeks' growth of *chia* seeds.

C

Chia Seeds

These tiny black seeds are from the lime-leaved sage plant, native to Mexico, and they were formerly used to make the oily, basic material for lacquer. *Chia* seeds are still considered to be the best material for making lacquer ware, but they have now been replaced largely by linseed oil for the craft.

An entirely different and unexpected use is made of *chia* seeds nowadays—it is a special way of growing the seeds, and children find the horticultural experience a fascinating one, which results in a "living" toy that amuses grownups as well as young people.

Red clay pottery armadillo with green-glazed head, surface scored to hold *chia* seeds. Made at Santa María Atzompa, Oaxaca. 5½″ × 2½″ (14 × 6.4 cm.)

The potters of the village of Santa María Atzompa, Oaxaca, make small animals of several kinds out of red clay: deer, dogs, armadillos and goats. The animals are formed by pressing soft clay into the two matching halves of a fired clay or plaster mold previously cast from an original clay model; in this way, from a number of molds, many little replicas of the different animals can be turned out in a day.

The animals are hollow and each has a one-half-inch hole at the highest point of its back. Before the newly-made form is dry, deep lengthwise scratches are made in the damp clay on the top and sides of the body, then the piece is dried in the sun. The bodies are not glazed, but the heads of the animals are dipped into a liquid, dark green glaze and the pieces are fired in the kiln. The finished red clay, green-headed *chia* seed animals are sold all over Mexico.

The buyer of the animal now mixes a small amount of *chia* seeds with water to make an oily, dark gray paste which is buttered all over the animal and smoothed into the scratches until the surface is covered. The body is then filled with water and the toy is set on a plate in case the water drips a little. Moisture seeps through the surface of the porous, unglazed clay and makes the seeds sprout. The toy must be kept filled with water, and in about five or six days tiny, gray sprouts will begin to appear. In ten days the red clay animal has grown a luxurious thick coat of slender stems, each with a tiny heart-shaped green leaf at its tip, making him look much fatter. His green head looks just right on the plump green body. In another week of growing, the armadillo begins to look more like a hedgehog, and the deer can barely see over his whiskers.

Chia seed animals are attractive even without their coats, but when the seed-growing procedure is followed, the creatures become a kind of silly but pretty adventure, especially for children. Looking at a *chia* seed animal in his full-blown coat is a good way to start the day with a laugh.

Red clay deer with green-glazed head, surface scored to hold *chia* seeds. Made at Santa María Atzompa, Oaxaca. 4¾″ × 5″ (12.1 × 12.7 cm.)

Red clay deer with a two weeks' growth of *chia* seeds.

84

Chickpeas

Small, inexpensive paper toys made for children for the Day of the Dead in November make use of this common vegetable to form the heads of miniature figures carrying a coffin in a funeral procession. The characteristic pointed knob on the chickpea is used to represent the nose of the heads of the figures—which are usually crowned with cotton hair and a paper cap. Inside the paper coffin carried by the robed pall-bearers is a corpse who also has a chickpea head.

Chicle

The dictionary defines chicle as a "gum obtained from the latex of the *sapodilla* tree which is used in the United States as the chief ingredient of chewing gum." Candy-coated Chiclets are chewed by the thousands in America, and there surely can be no North American child who hasn't popped a balloon of bubble gum.

Chicle is said to have been chewed first more than a thousand years ago by the Mayan Indians of Yucatán. Most chicle comes from Guatemala; in Mexico it is produced in Talpa de Allende, Jalisco, and in Tenosique, Tabasco, but it is not cultivated extensively for export. The material, unlikely as it may seem, is now sometimes used by Indian artisans for making miniature objects—and even that craft is beginning to disappear.

The latex is obtained by tapping the *sapodilla* tree; connected V-shaped cuts are made in the bark the whole length of the trunk of the tree, and the liquid oozes out and flows into a container at the bottom of the tree. The extracted milky latex is boiled to thicken it and when cool, it is kneaded to remove excess water. The thick, whitish chicle can be tinted by kneading vegetable colors into the dough.

Artisans use chicle for making small, decorative miniature objects. The tinted chicle is warmed again and rolled into fine strands, and because the gum is so elastic, these can be woven into tiny baskets. The gum is also formed into small plates of fruit or baskets of flowers, and shaped into dolls and miniature bird cages. In Talpa de Allende, beautiful small replicas of the sculpture of the town's patroness Virgin are made of chicle.

The material hardens, but the delicate objects made from it are very fragile. Collectors treasure chicle pieces and display them as they would porcelain figurines, which they do in fact resemble.

Funeral procession—colored paper; figures in clerical robes with chick-pea heads and cotton hair carrying a coffin on the Day of the Dead. Inside the coffin is a small corpse made of the same materials. Length 6⅝", width 4¾", height 3½" (16.8 × 12.1 × 8.9 cm.)

Miniature pitcher made of rolled strips of chicle gum, painted decoration. Height 1⅜" (3.5 cm.)

Clay

Clay is the age-old material used for making the pottery of Mexico—one of the country's most distinctive popular arts—and the handmade clay toys have a charm all their own. Pottery toys include: *nacimiento* figures for Christmas, Trees of Life, whistles, piggy banks, dolls, puppets, figures of men, women and children, realistic and fanciful animals, birds, surrealist constructions, skulls, skeletons, small merry-go-rounds with riders, mermaids, bells, peace doves, *chia* seed animals, miniature pots, bowls, dishes, pitchers and tea sets.

Pottery clay is simply earth of a pliable consistency; an abundant supply in many areas of the country means that it is inexpensive to use. Pottery villages have grown up near the sites of natural clay deposits. The potter first digs his clay, then he mixes it with a certain amount of water and kneads or "wedges" it thoroughly by hand until it is workable. Then he is ready to begin working at his craft.

Shaping

A potter can shape his clay into any form because of its natural plasticity. Pottery can be built up by hand in several ways: by *coiling*, by rolling out *slabs* of clay, or it can be made by joining and smoothing *pinched*-off bits and hunks of the material. In most countries a potter's wheel—a small, horizontal platform that turns—is used to shape the clay by hand as it turns; this method is called *throwing*.

In Mexico, the only sort of wheel used—and it is seen very seldom—is simply two round-bottomed fired clay saucers with the bottoms together. The top saucer holds the clay and this is rotated by the potter by twirling it around as it balances on the bottom of the other, inverted saucer. The skill required to keep the top saucer centered, and to shape the clay at the same time is an amazing balancing act. This method is used in San Bartólo Coyotepec, the black pottery village of Oaxaca.

Mold-casting

When replicas of a piece are desirable a negative mold is made in two or more pieces from an original hand-shaped model. The molds in Mexico are usually made of clay and fired; sometimes they are made of plaster.

Rolled-out slabs of moist clay are pressed into the two matching halves of a mold, and when the clay is dry enough to hold its shape, the halves are removed from the mold and stuck together with more wet clay to form the whole piece. Details may then be added by hand. Small doll and animal bodies are hollow when made this way. All toy rattles, piggy banks and whistles, whatever their size or shape, must be hollow in order for them to work.

Clay replicas can also be made in piece-molds by pouring liquid clay (slip) into a mold that is tied together and has an opening at one end. When the slip has lost enough moisture so that it forms a wall inside the mold (usually the more absorbent plaster, in this case) excess liquid clay is poured out leaving a hollow casting. Then the mold is taken apart, the whole cast is taken out, trimmed and smoothed and set aside to dry. The surface of mold-cast pieces can, of course, be textured or decorated in the same way as the hand-formed pieces.

Black piggy bank made of burnished black clay at San Bartólo Coyotepec, Oaxaca. Length 3½" (8.9 cm.)

86

Five miniature nested pottery bowls, red clay with edges decorated with white tempera paint; varnished. Diameter of largest bowl 3¼" (8.3 cm.)

Surface Texture

After pots and other objects are formed, they may be left plain or they can be decorated by applying small pieces of soft clay to the surface (*pastillaje*) or the surface can be carved, pierced or incised with a tool. Toymakers sometimes use punches or sticks to indent marks for eyes, hair, whiskers, fingers and claws on their little clay figures.

Colored decorations or coatings

Color may be applied to pottery in several ways, either before or after the piece is fired in a kiln. Colored slip or glazes can be painted on with a brush, or a whole piece may be dipped into a liquid colored clay or glaze. Slips add color to clay pieces, and glazes add both color and a protective, glossy finish. Cooking pots are glazed inside to make them "wet-proof."

An easily-applied, colorful decoration may be painted on *fired* unglazed pottery with ordinary tempera water colors, and many Mexican clay toys are enlivened and finished in this simple way. The colors are not really permanent and may rub off in time. Painted pieces are sometimes given a coat of ordinary varnish and this will protect the colors and make the surface shiny. The villages of Ocotlán, Oaxaca and Acatlán, Puebla are known for their tempera-decorated, unvarnished toys and pottery.

All clay pieces—hand-formed, mold-cast, plain or decorated—ranging in size from a tiny clay bead no larger than a pea to a large cooking pot—must be allowed to dry thoroughly. Then they are baked or fired in a kiln in order for the clay to become hard and durable.

Firing

In Mexico the outdoor kilns are very simple and cannot be heated to a very high temperature. Most native Mexican pottery can be described as low-fired,

Kiln being fired below ground; smoke can be seen escaping through the shards stacked on top of the kiln. Santa María Atzompa, Oaxaca.

Kiln constructed and fired on the ground level; Santa María Atzompa, Oaxaca.

though commercial ceramic factories in the country do turn out some fine high-fired wares.

Most country kilns are built directly on the ground or are underground chambers lined with brick and fired from a pit underneath. The dried pots are stacked into the kiln through the open top, and when filled the kiln is covered over with shards of previously-fired clay to keep the heat in.

Fuel for the kiln is wood, reed, grass, straw, corncobs, dried dung, and any available material that will burn. After the firing, which may take several hours, the kiln is allowed to cool, the covering is removed and the finished pieces are taken out. Many Mexican pots, small sculptures and toys are left in their plain earth color—buff, red, brown or black. The color is determined by the chemicals in the clay, and sometimes by the way it is fired.

Mexican children as potters

In a pottery village where literally everyone is engaged in some phase of the making of clay objects, all the children start learning the craft at the age of seven or eight. Soft, squishy clay is their plaything.

In the black pottery village of Coyotepec, Oaxaca, the children make many kinds of beads, and many are carefully hand-modeled small birds, stars and other shapes. The strings of beads are a favorite purchase of visitors to the shops and patio potteries.

In Atzompa, children learn to make the miniature animal musicians—one of the characteristic wares of that village. Also, a child's tiny fingers are useful to form the miniature pots with a dark green glaze that are sold in strings of a dozen in Oaxaca market stalls; some of these little treasures are made by children.

Some young potters and their parents in the Oaxaca City area who have acquired enough skill to copy small clay pieces engage in the nefarious business of making fake artifacts. The pieces are fired, then buried in the ground around the tombs of Monte Alban—to "age" archeologically—and then they are miraculously found and dug up by the child who offers the little antiques for sale to tourists. This harmless game goes on at many historic sites in Mexico.

Pottery Villages

The wares and toys turned out by artisans living in one pottery village of Mexico will almost invariably be made in the distinctive style of that village, and no

Small copper pots, pans and bell, with copper wire handles. Pieces are hand-hammered at Santa Clara del Cobre. Large pot with handle 1¾″ tall, bell 1⅛″ tall (4.4 and 2.9 cm.)

Copper

other. In Oaxaca, noted for its pottery, work from Santa María Atzompa is either reddish clay without a glaze, or red clay glazed in dark green—no other color. Atzompa cooking pots and bowls are usually red bisque on the outside and glazed dark green inside. Work made in Ocotlán is red or buff clay painted with bright tempera decorations; San Bartólo Coyotepec wares are always black and are sometimes burnished with a stone to give them a smooth, subtle gloss. This rubbing technique was used centuries ago, before fired glazes were known. Each village tradition is continued year after year.

There are, of course, a number of Mexican potters whose work is distinctive, as in all of the arts anywhere; some are known internationally, and these men and women are highly respected by their countrymen. But even these master potters use the same clay as their fellow-villagers and finish their pots in the same general way.

The craft of soldering and hand-hammering *cobre* to make decorative containers, candlesticks, etc. is said to have been taught to the natives by a Spanish bishop in the sixteenth century. The Tarascan Indians living in the high mountains of Michoacán carry on the craft almost exclusively in one small village named *Santa Clara del Cobre,* also called *Villa Escalante,* or roughly: "village climbing a ladder." Skilled metal workers hammer out handsome copper plates, trays, urns, vases, pots, cups, mugs, pitchers and bells which are sold all over Mexico. All have the characteristic subtle hammer marks in the metal achieved only by hand forming. The styles still have another-century look, and no contemporary styles seem to have developed.

Artisans in the village specialize in making tiny copper miniatures of all the same objects. The work of making a very small copper vase or pitcher is in some ways even more difficult than producing the larger pieces. Santa Clara copper miniatures are also widely marketed and are very popular. They can be found in enough shapes and small sizes to gratify the most discriminating collector.

89

Corn Shucks

Corn is grown everywhere in Mexico—in country fields, in town gardens and on the mountain terraces; it is the life-sustaining food of the country where it is fed to cattle and where millions of *tortillas* made from the grain are eaten by the people every day. Corn has dozens of other uses as food so there is always a plentiful supply of the outer leaves of the ears of corn—the shucks or husks. These are used to wrap tamales.

Country Indian children improvise dolls out of bundles of corn shucks tied together in various ways, and they sometimes make smaller dolls out of corn cobs, dressed in husks or rags and decorated with flowers.

Another kind of corn shuck doll is the smaller, more or less professionally-made "character" doll with clothing of husks carefully cut and made to represent people of various occupations in Mexico. These beautiful little dolls are about five or six inches tall (12.7–15.3 cm.) and stand on a small wood base; they are collected by doll fanciers and lovers of miniatures, and are not really a toy. Some even smaller miniature dolls are made of corn husks, and these are no taller than a common pin. Corn shucks can be dyed, so some of the small figures are very colorful.

Corn shucks are also used to make the traditional Corpus Christi *mulito*, or the little mule that appears every year about the middle of June as a symbol of this important festival. (See chapter V—June.)

Corn shuck doll, stuffed with grasses and painted blue, purple, red and yellow. Height 15¾" (40 cm.)

Cotton

This fluffy white stuff is used by toymakers to form the hair and beards of miniature figures made of clay, wood and paper; it is the favorite wig for small skeletons made for the Day of the Dead.

Miniature painted clay figure of old woman skeleton selling bananas in the market; cotton hair. Height 1¾" (4.4 cm.)

90

F

Feathers

Tropical birds of all kinds supplied the feathers that were used to make ceremonial robes of "feather mosaic" worn by tribal leaders in the Mexico of earlier centuries. In the nineteenth and early twentieth centuries there was a vogue for intricate pictures made out of feathers, but these have disappeared entirely.

Mexican artisans find use for feathers in making some toys and costumes of today. Feathers are used for hair and headdresses on puppets, (See color plate) for making little papier mâché cocks used for a "cockfight" toy, on masks of various kinds, and to top woven palm-leaf rattles. The colorful Feather Dance performed by Indians in the State of Oaxaca depends for its drama upon the large, brightly-colored plumed headdresses worn by the dancers.

Birds of the tropical jungles in Guatemala provide most of the feathers used in Mexico today.

Fibers

The leaves of three similar, spiky-leaved plants native to Central America—*ixtle, maguey* and *henequen*—are used to make a sisal—or hemp-like fiber that can be made into rope and woven into a rough cloth. Toymakers find it very useful as realistic tails for papier mâché animals, as whiskers for masks, and for weaving doll hats, tiny baskets, bridles, purses and miniature sandals and mats.

Flowers

Flowers and flower petals are used in many imaginative and decorative ways in Mexico. Flower petal designs are painstakingly laid down on church plazas on special occasions in patterns and designs of Indian origin. Floats and litters carried in religious processions are often covered entirely with flowers. Tiny "everlasting" dried flowers are used to decorate papier mâché birds; and the flamboyant paper flowers of Mexico are world-famous.

Flowers—roses made of crêpe paper, multicolor.

Two baskets; left: woven of *ixtle* or *maguey* fiber, right: woven of palm in natural color and dyed red and green. Heights, without handles: 1⅜″ and ¹¹/₁₆″ (3.5, 1.7 cm.)

Flowers—carnations made of crêpe paper, multicolor.

91

Bull—clear hand-blown or "stretched" glass, made in Guadalajara, Jalisco. Height 2⅝" (6.7 cm.)

G

Glass

Mexican hand-blown glass is famous for its glowing colors and its distinctive hand-crafted look. Most Mexican glass is made in Guadalajara, Jalisco, and this city is known as the center of this comparatively small but thriving industry. In addition to their other wares, glass craftsmen make many kinds of delicate miniatures and they are to be found in most collections of fine small crafts. Blown or "stretched" glass animals, vases, goblets, intricate candelabras and other tiny masterpieces are made in Guadalajara and sold in shops all across Mexico.

Glitter

This modern material—powdered metallic tinsel—is sprinkled on the fresh paint of masks and toys, and used also to brighten the robes of *nacimiento* figures. Even though it is not edible, silver glitter is often used to decorate *alfeñique* sugar-paste figures.

Gourds

Dried gourds with hard seeds that make a pleasant rattling noise when the gourd is shaken are used in Mexico as an important part of many Indian dances. Tiny gourds are given to babies as safe, durable playthings, and the seeds of gourds are used as rattlers in woven palm leaf rattles and in the pre-Hispanic pottery turtle toy.

Miniature gourds are carefully painted or decorated in a lacquer technique for the shelves and cabinets of collectors both young and old.

L

Lacquer

Lacquer work has been famed as one of the arts of Mexico since Spanish colonial times. The craft is said to have been brought to New Spain by Chinese craftsmen. In the seventeenth and eighteenth centuries Mexican lacquerware was one of the finest arts of the country. The beautiful, large lacquer trays (*bateas*) and wooden chests of that era are now museum pieces.

Tiny ram and lamb made of *alfeñique* sugar paste, decorated with silver glitter for an altar decoration on the Day of the Dead. Ram is 2¼" high, lamb 1" (5.7 and 2.5 cm.)

There are three kinds of lacquer work:

1. Inlaid (*embrutido* or *encrustado*) which is the most complicated and highly regarded. The wood is given many coats of lacquer (a thick compound of powdered dolomite, color and oil) and each layer is carefully smoothed and burnished. Then the design is scratched or cut through the few top layers of the base lacquer, and other lacquer colors are rubbed into the cuts or cut-out areas—or *inlaid*—into the lacquer base coat. The whole is then polished and oiled until it is smooth and glossy.

2. Incised or grooved lacquer (*rayado*) in which the wood is given several coats of lacquer, usually bright red or green. Then, on top of the polished color the piece is given several more coats of *black* lacquer. Each coat is rubbed down to a smooth, glossy finish. The design is then cut through, or *grooved* through the black, just deeply enough to reveal the colored layer. Sometimes the coats of lacquer are applied in reverse order—first black, then red or green. The final effect will be essentially the same, except that the final coat will always stand out in a delicate bas relief above the first coats. The finished tray, box, gourd, panel or chest is then polished to a high gloss with oil and cotton.

3. Painted (*aplicado* or *dorado*) lacquer is simply the painting of colored designs of flowers, birds, etc. with oil paints on a base of several coats of lacquer. This is the simplest and least complicated of the techniques, and the one that is now most apt to be practiced by unskilled artisans.

In recent years the various time-consuming and exacting methods used to make fine lacquer are becoming less and less used and the craft is dying out, or is being considerably downgraded in quality.

As might be expected, Mexican miniatures in lacquer are still made and are still treasured. There are small chests, trays and masks that are quite well done, and lacquered and painted gourds in many colors that are for collectors, or to be used as babies' rattles.

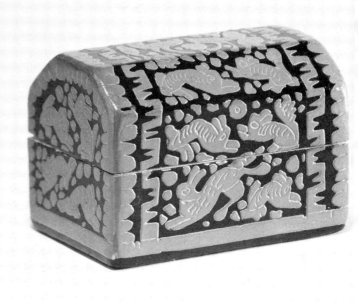

Small lacquer chest, green and black; made by the *rayado* technique with traditional animal motifs. 2⅝″ × 1¾″ × 1¾″ (6.7 × 4.4 × 4.4 cm.)

Two tiny painted gourd rattles and small top. Round rattle is 1⅛″ in diameter, the top 1½″ (2.9; 3.8 cm.)

Lead soldiers on horseback, carrying pistols; painted with touches of red and green. Height 1⅜″ (3.5 cm.)

Lead

Lead soldiers were a favorite toy of Victorian days, and they were imported by the army-load from Europe into Mexico where their popularity continues. Lead is a metal that melts at a very low temperature and is therefore easy to melt and cast. Master models for lead toys are carved in wood, or formed in clay or plaster, and from those originals two-piece sand-cast molds are made in brass or iron. These are hinged at one edge and each mold has an opening at the top or at one end. The mold is closed, clamped and the molten lead is simply poured into the opening. Lead cools in a few minutes, and when the mold is opened, presto! there is the toy. One mold can be used to cast scores of toys in a few hours. Cast lead can be painted with enamels to color the uniforms of soldiers, and to paint colored details on other pieces.

In Mexico there are stores that have a case full of lead soldiers and other lead miniatures such as: "silverware", plates, cups, goblets, bowls, candlesticks, swords, sabres, guns, vases, combs, mirrors, skeletons, flower bouquets and pots and pans, none more than an inch or two in size. Some pieces that can be bought today are undoubtedly cast in the identical metal molds that were used generations ago.

Leather

The handcrafted and tooled leather work of Mexico is well-known, and many travelers go away carrying their belongings in handmade luggage. One can buy beautiful saddles, boots, belts, sandals, tooled purses and portfolios as well as tailored leather jackets and hats in many of the larger cities of Mexico.

The same craftsmen who make fine leather goods turn their skills to the making of miniature boots, saddles, purses and *huaraches,* and these are collected by both children and adults as toys or as small artifacts for the treasure shelf.

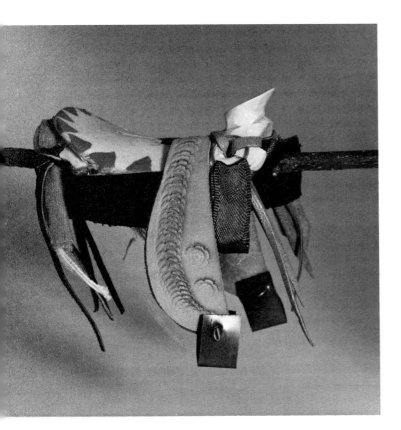

Saddle made of leather, wood, cloth and metal—a reproduction of a *charro* saddle. Length 3½″ (8.9 cm.)

94

M

Masks

Mexicans have used masks since pre-Hispanic days and the codices show figures of gods, priests and ritual dancers wearing them. Masks were sometimes put on idols and on effigies of the dead. The most ancient masks are archeological treasures and are covered with mosaics of shells, obsidian, jade and turquoise, and some have real hair and teeth. Wooden masks were carved to represent the gods, often as animal faces, and sorcerers wore them in ceremonies honoring pagan deities and to invoke magic.

In more recent years in remote areas primitive wooden masks were also made to identify the officials of a village and were hung on their dwellings as a badge of authority; such masks were worn only on the most important local occasions.

Traditional dances of many Indian tribes in Mexico still use masks as an elemental part of their colorful costumes. The Yaquis and Mayos of Sonora wear distinctive wooden dance masks and many folkloric dances are never performed without their distinctive false faces. For the dances of *Los Negritos*— the little negroes, and the dance of *Los Viejitos*— the little old men, young boy dancers depend upon masks for the humor and effectiveness of their performance. A famous dance performed principally in Guerrero is that of the battle of the Moors and Christians, for which the dancers wear large masks and fancy costumes and carry wooden swords with which they fight their battles.

Devil masks, all kinds of animal faces and the Tiger mask of Olinalá representing the jaguar are worn in many places for pageants and dances during fiestas. Carnival costumes are made of everything from burlap to satin and are decorated with bells, ribbons, paper streamers, tinsel and what not. Carnival participants are usually the ordinary village people and they never seem to grow tired as they continue their antics all through a day and sometimes through two or three days, encased in a disguise from head to foot. (See color plates)

Mask, papier maché, painted with pink and white tempera and metallic gold; worn by young boys for the "Dance of the Little Old Men." 7″ × 7½″ (17.8 × 19.1 cm.)

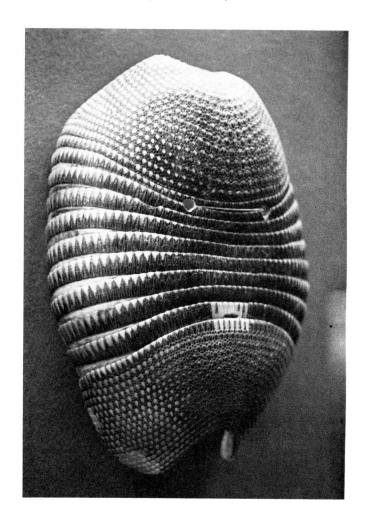

Mask made of an armadillo shell with two eye-holes and a mouth indicated by knotted palm strips. Probably an unusual dance mask, not ceremonial.

Turtle and piglet, made of a walnut and a pecan shell. Made at Guanajuato City. Height ¾″ (1.9 cm.)

N

Nutshells

Some of the most unusual miniature toys of Mexico are made almost exclusively by the prisoners in the jail of Guanajuato City. These skilled men use nutshells: walnuts, pecans, acorns and shells of other native nuts to make some miniscule ornaments that are probably unique. The dried nutshells are cut into sections, the contents are removed, then the shell is put back together again with the sections hinged and latched with fine copper wire and scraps of metal beer cans, so that the little "doors" open and close neatly. Inside, all kinds of incredibly tiny scenes are made with clay, lace, netting, cloth, toothpicks, paper, paint, tinsel and glue. One shell may contain a bride and groom about ⅜ of an inch tall (9 cm.); the members of the wedding party are standing inside of the "doors" of the nutshell. Another nut may contain a market scene with four or five vendors and their wares. These ornaments have a wire loop and thread hanger at the top, and many travelers buy them to use as Christmas tree ornaments.

Some of the scenic nutshell miniatures have wooden heads and feet of birds added to the nutshell, so that when they are closed they are complete small standing sculptures that can be opened.

The artisan-prisoners also make acorn "pigs" with a wobbly tail and ears and a removable cork nose. When a live fly is entrapped inside, the pig's ears and tail move as long as the fly is moving. A tiny, fat nutshell turtle is made with carved wooden feet, tail and head—and the tail and head are movable so that they swing from side to side at the slightest touch.

These strange miniatures are a real curiosity and are sold mostly in the streets and plazas of only two towns—Guanajuato and the neighboring San Miguel de Allende—by young boys and girls, who may be the children of the prisoners.

Judas figure, the devil—a doll-sized representation of the betrayer of Christ; a traditional Holy Saturday toy. Height 9″ (22.9 cm.)

Piñata—peacock—*pavo real*—an unusually large and beautifully-made example of this art, made especially for this book. The body is formed around an *olla,* the long tail feathers are made of carefully-cut, scored and folded tissue paper decorated with foil spots. The whole is covered with incredibly fine-cut ruffles and decorated with streamers cut by the grandmother of the Vasquez family of San Miguel de Allende. Height 40″, length 54″ (1.02 m. × 1.37 m.)

Piñata—yellow turkey (?) with a rainbow-colored tissue paper fanned tail. A Vasquez family bird—the makers of the masterpieces of Mexican piñatas, San Miguel de Allende. Height 28″ (71.1 cm.)

The Three Kings—bearers of Epiphany gifts to the children of Mexico—riding on an elephant, a camel and a horse. Carved wood, painted in aniline colors. The group forms an impressive caravan. Lengths 7¾″, widths about 3″ and heights about 7½″ (19.7, 7.6 and 19.1 cm.)

Organ cactus—*organo*—growing wild in the countryside near Etla, Oaxaca.

Torito—little bull—the star performer in the fireworks bull fight staged by the fireworks makers of Mexico, and an important part of fiestas everywhere. This charmingly naive *torito* was made by seventy-year-old Cirilo Salvador of Oaxaca City. Height of bull 27″, length 43″, width 26″ (68.6 × 109.2 × 66 cm.) Overall height with fireworks superstructure 44″ (1.12 m.)

The same *torito* shooting off in a whole new explosion of green color and yellow shooting sparks.

Cirilo Salvador's *torito* shooting off—in this case standing on the ground; not carried by the *cohetero* for the crowd. A red flare momentarily lights the scene.

Modern punched and painted tin Christmas tree with candle holders
soldered to the branches. A holiday ornament whose source is far from
Mexico. Height 13¾" (35 cm.)

Country cemetery at Etla, Oaxaca on November
3rd; graves are covered with *zempasúchitl,* flowers
of the dead. Native "organ" cactus planted at the
head of the grave makes a dignified monument in
keeping with the modest roadside cemetery.

Punched and pierced tin Christmas ornaments painted with aniline colors. Height 3″ and 4″ (7.6 and 10.2 cm.)

Day of the Dead ornamental figure of a skeleton in a sombrero, blowing a golden horn. Papier mâché over wire, painted with tempera colors. Height 10½″ (26.7 cm.)

Piñata—the simplest and probably most common version of Mexico's famous Christmas ornaments or game accessories; six-pointed star formed over a round clay pot, with foil points and star in the center and tissue paper ruffles and streamers. Made by the Vasquez family of San Miguel de Allende: Ricardo, Narcisso, Carmen, Florentina and Juana with help from grandmother Juana Spinoza Vasquez. Width 42″ (1.07 m.)

Palm ornaments made for children to carry into church to be blessed on Palm Sunday. The sun ornament on handle is 5″ in diameter (12.7 cm.) The other two, dyed red and green, are 12″ long (30.5 cm.)

P

Palm Leaves

The palm tree with its long, pointed dark green leaves is a graceful part of the Mexican landscape, and the tough, slender leaves are put to so many uses, both practical and decorative that it is impossible to imagine the country without its *palmas*.

Palm leaves are waterproof as well as tough and fibrous and when they are green they can be woven, folded, twisted and tied securely. The leaf can be split lengthwise into strips that are strong enough to be woven, even if they are no wider than a cord. The green of the leaves turns to a pale gold color as it dries and is shiny and handsome when used for objects and ornaments of many kinds.

Along with *carrizo* and *tule*—reed and rush—palm leaves are used to make *petates*, the sturdy woven mat that serves Mexicans as a bed, rug, wall-covering, sunshade, umbrella, wrapper for market goods, table mat, beach towel and shroud. Gardeners scoop up and carry their trash in a *petate* exactly like the clean one they sleep on at night. There is probably no man-made object as universally useful anywhere in the world as is the Mexican *petate*.

Mexican farmer with a sickle taking refuge from a storm in his hut, wearing a palm-leaf rain cape.

Palm leaf man with burro, both carrying pineapples; natural and green-dyed. 3¾″ × 3½″ (9.5 × 8.9 cm.)

Palm leaves are woven to make decorative symbols for Palm Sunday, fans, hats and baskets. The split, dried leaves can be dyed with aniline colors (usually red or green) to make attractive, patterned woven objects like table mats, purses and cigarette cases. The leaves also serve as thatching for adobe house roofs and are sewn together in layers to make a serviceable and cost-free rain cape for farmers.

Many toys are made of woven palm leaves: the Corpus Christi *mulito* (which is also made in many sizes, in addition to the corn shuck toy) (see Chapter V—June), figures and animals of all kinds, some miniscule and some almost life-sized, rattles decorated with feathers and miniature figures in great variety.

Paper

The first colored and printed papers and delicate foils made of metallic leaf reached Mexico via Spain from the Orient in the 17th or 18th century. Since then, Mexican craftsmen have found dozens of uses for paper as a material for handcrafted objects and decorations.

In the nineteenth and early twentieth century the neighborhood drinking establishments were the *pulquerías,* where a potent, cheap liquor called *pulque* made from the native *maguey* plant was sold. In spite of the reputedly unhealthy influence of such places, the Mexican *pulquerías*—now almost non-existent— were invariably gaily decorated across the doorways and from wall to wall inside with festoons of cut-out tissue paper banners in many colors. The walls inside and outside the tiny bars were painted with murals spontaneously done by untutored neighborhood artists who wanted to make the *pulquería* the most glorious place in the village. The paper banners and the paintings often accomplished just that.

98

Readily available cheap cardboard, corrugated board, wrapping paper, newspaper, crêpe paper, tissue paper and foil are all used today in Mexico with imagination and skill. The heavier boards and papers are used to build up and reenforce many paper constructions like *piñatas* and papier mâché figures.

Foil papers are used to make tinsel bouquets of dramatic size for religious occasions, and to decorate wagons and litters pulled and carried in processions. Large papier mâché figures are sometimes completely covered with colored foil instead of being painted, and Mexicans of all ages love the shiny, metallic colors. Metal foils are also used for cut-out paper decorations, pinwheels, Christmas and New Years greetings, and as accents on carnival heads, masks and papier mâché toys.

Tissue paper is a favorite material of Mexican artisans and toymakers. It is called *papel de seda* (silk paper) or *papel China,* from the days of its first importation, and it can be bought by the single sheet in any paper shop for a fraction of a peso. Because of this, the poorest child can buy a sheet of colorful paper for making something of her or his own creation.

Tissue paper is used to make the ruffles on *piñatas,* for kites and aerial balloons, flowers, garlands made in combination with wheat straw and for colorful, delicate paper-link chains which festoon many plazas from tree to tree and corner to corner at the Christmas season. Fiesta banquet tables are decorated with cut-out tissue paper mats, little bouquets of cut tissue paper flags and foil cut-outs. A whole village at fiesta time is strung with fluttery, small cut-paper banners in many colors.

Crêpe paper and tissue paper are both used to make Mexico's flourishing crop of paper flowers, which are to be found decorating everything from hotel lobbies to country church altars and shrines in simple farm huts. Crêpe paper is also used for the decorative details of tissue paper kites, *piñatas* and fireworks figures.

Paper—a mundane material in most countries—goes far to make Mexico a festive place.

Red, blue and silver foil pinwheel on a stick. Diameter 4¼″ (10.8 cm.)

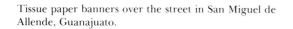

Tissue paper banners over the street in San Miguel de Allende, Guanajuato.

99

Papier maché carnival heads in various stages of construction in the workshop of Guadalupe Rodriguez at San Miguel de Allende, Guanajuato.

Papier Mâché

This plastic material, to which we give a French name, is called *papel majada* in Spanish, which means pounded or pulverized paper. This is not a complete description of it, for in Mexico paper is very often simply torn into pieces and soaked in paste for the craft, so it is also called *papel pegado*, or pasted paper.

There are two traditional ways and one more modern way of working with this simple and inexpensive modeling material, and the size of the piece to be made largely determines the method to be used. One traditional way is used to make large carnival figures, heads, Judases and *piñatas*; each object is individually made and is an *original*. A framework or skeleton for the piece is made of thin, split reeds or wood strips, bent and shaped as necessary, and tied together with cords; the framework must accurately delineate the figure. This is a tricky sculptural problem and not an easy task to accomplish. (*Piñatas* are made a little differ-

ently, and that process is described separately below.) After the all-important reed, bamboo or wood skeleton is made, the artisan uses heavy brown paper—discarded cement bags are a favorite material—or newspaper torn into pieces and soaked in a thickish flour and water paste. To this, for some unknown reason, a little lime juice is sometimes added. The paste-covered pieces of paper are plastered over the skeleton one by one, and gradually the form appears. Before long a surprisingly sturdy shape is built up in layers of paper, and the paste (and the paper) will finally dry very hard. When the basic shape is established, cardboard, corrugated board or newspaper is rolled up, cut, shaped or pasted together to make noses, ears, hands, hat brims, wings, tails and horns and these are attached to the body with pasted paper tabs and become part of the figure. When the piece is almost dry it is sometimes finished by being covered with colored paper or foil; or when

100

completely dry it is painted—usually with tempera water colors. The finished pieces are extremely light because of their hollow construction, but they are hard-surfaced and not as fragile as they seem.

A second traditional method is used to make smaller pieces: papier mâché masks, small Judases, dolls and animal toys. Most small pieces need to be duplicated many times and so the process is quite different. First, a clay model is made which looks exactly like the figure wanted—doll, animal or what-not. Then a fired clay or plaster mold is made from that model, and it is usually cast in two or more pieces that join perfectly. The hardened "master" piece-mold can then be used to make countless replicas of the papier mâché object. The paper to be used in a mold is torn up into much smaller pieces than those for the framework construction of the larger pieces. The scraps are then sometimes mashed and mixed into the paste with a beater or electric mixer (if there is electricity), so this is really pulverized *papel majado*.

The wet paper is pressed into the mold in five or six layers (if in small pieces), or in a thin, even coating (if a pulp.) Each open half or part of the mold containing the wet paper mixture is allowed to become partly dry. Then, the almost-hard matching halves of the piece are taken out of the mold and patched together with more pasted paper to make a firm, whole doll or animal. This mold method explains why papier mâché toys are very simply modeled without much detail. A complicated shape would be hard to pull out of the piece-mold. Details are usually indicated by being painted on later. Sometimes paper ears or rope tails are stuck on after the cast has hardened. In the case of a doll with jointed arms and legs, each arm and leg is made in its own little two-piece clay mold in the same way as the body. The two halves of cast paper shapes are pasted together to make whole, hollow arms and legs. Then the finished and hardened paper pieces are painted and perforated so as to insert the connecting cords. (See color plate)

If a Papier mâché craftsman knows that he may be required to make several large carnival figures or images, he may decide it is worth his while to make large fired clay or plaster molds in several pieces that can be used more than once, by using the method described above. Light reenforcement with reed strips inside the individual pieces after they have almost hardened, but before they are put together will make the piece strong, and the artisan has saved himself the work of constructing an individual framework for each figure.

Wooden angel, carved and painted, natural wood, black and wearing a purple robe; the wings appear to be upside down. Height 5½″ (14 cm.)

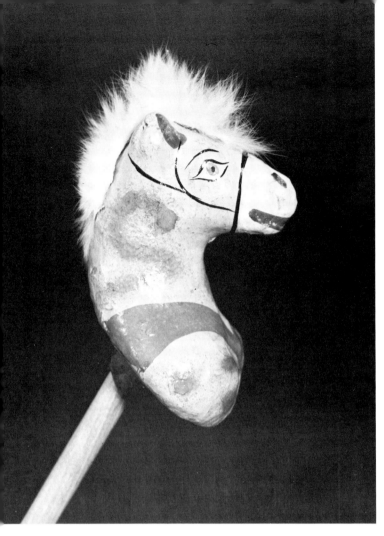

Horse's head on a stick, painted papier maché; yellow, red and black with white rabbit fur mane. Height of head 6" (15.2 cm.)

There is still a third way to use papier mâché for making small objects. It is a method of forming actual-sized fruits and vegetables used as table ornaments and often seen in fine shops in Mexico. First, the orange, pomegranate or whatever it may be is modeled in clay or carved in wood. Then this model is oiled or soaped and wet papier maché is pasted to the whole outside of the model. When the coating is thick enough and has hardened, a cut is made with a sharp knife around the entire circumference of the papier mâché shell, and the two halves are removed. Then they are put back together again, the seams are pasted over with more paper, and the hollow object is left to dry. These attractive and slightly unreal-looking fruits and vegetables are painted in bright tempera colors and varnished, and they make a very pretty table decoration in a Mexican basket or bowl.

Papier mâché is used to make carnival figures, giant heads, religious images, piñatas, fireworks figures, horses' heads on sticks, skeletons, skulls, masks, Judas figures, animals of every description, dolls, rattles and other toys. The inexpensive material and the rather simple molding procedure mean that Mexican folk art shops are often—especially at holiday time—filled to bursting with papier mâché toys that most families can afford to buy for their children. The fact that every toy, no matter how simple, is hand painted at the whim of the artist means that colors are extremely varied, and no two faces, dresses or suits are quite alike. A horse may be painted pink, red, orange or purple, and therefore looks like a *different* horse. Each jointed, tinsel-decorated lady doll from Celaya has her own name painted on her belly, and the child chooses the one that looks and sounds the prettiest.

R

Rabbit Fur

The fur of this domestic animal—the meat of which is used for food in Mexico—is used to make white, gray brown or black "fur" of toy wood animals and monkey jumping jacks.

Rabbit-fur monkey jumping jack operated by a cord. The fur is glued to a wooden figure and the face is made of clay, painted brown. Made in the State of Chiapas. Figure is 7½" tall (19.1 cm.)

Reed, Bamboo and Cane

The Spanish word for reed is *carrizo,* but it is also called "Mexican Bamboo." Since *carrizo, bambú* and *caña* (cane) are so much alike, we group them here as one. These mature, jointed, hollow plant stalks are used by Mexican artisans to make everything from kites to furniture, and reed has become an almost indispensable material. Dry reeds are very tough to cut crosswise, even with a sharp saw, but are comparatively easy to split lengthwise. Constructions made of *carrizo* are usually notched and fitted together, woven or fastened with cord or wire, as the stuff is too hard and pieces are too curved to be glued, nailed or screwed together like wood. A delicate, split bamboo piece is light but strong, and a large, well-made bamboo basket can be used like a barrel to carry the heaviest of loads. A list of some of the toys and decorations partly or wholly made of bamboo in Mexico includes: *castillos, piñatas,* papier mâché carnival figures, the huge Judases of the past and the smaller ones of the present, fireworks *toritos,* clowns, turtles and dolls, kites, bird cages and baskets

Children use *carrizo* to make flutes and whistles, and as playtime horses, swords, whips and guns. Their parents use it for the woven *petate* mats that serve dozens of household and other purposes, for fences, for roof-supports, table tops and poles to hold up their canvas sunshades at the market.

Pair of small, cheap Judas figures with fireworks, made of reed and colored tissue paper and rolled-up newspaper; colors: green, purple, orange and white. These little figures are stuck in the ground or in a flower pot to be shot off, and are the miniscule remnants of the once common giant Judas figures used to celebrate Holy Saturday, the day before Easter. Height 15″ (38.1 cm.) *From the collection of Jean and Russell Ames.*

Reed bird cage put together without nails or glue. Mexicans love birds and this kind of cage holds a singing pet in almost every patio in the country—sometimes six or eight of them. Length 8⅞″, depth 6⅞″, height 11½″ (22.5 × 17.5 × 29.2 cm.)

Nacimiento in the home of the tin-makers, the Velasco family in Oaxaca. The scene begins in a small niche in the right wall, and trails onto a three-step platform, with many figurines. All the dark areas are Spanish moss. The crèche appears to remain set up all year around in a roofed part of the patio, next to the tin-working area.

Ornament made of natural wheat straw with grain-heads attached, called *Corazon de Trigo*—heart of wheat; a traditional design, cleverly made and said to be a fertility symbol. Width 8″ (20.3 cm.)

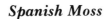

S

Spanish Moss

This smoky, growing plant that drapes itself and sometimes almost enwraps trees in gray-green festoons in the country is a readily-available material for use in Mexican Christmas *nacimientos* or crêches. No self-respecting maker of a crêche would think of constructing his or her Christmas scene without moss, and the Biblical figures in city plaza *nacimientos* are almost drowned in a sea of it. No need for city people to search for growing moss—it is sold in bundles for five centavos in the markets from December 16th to December 24th.

Straw

The same wheat grain that is a valuable food crop all over the world is grown in the fertile valleys and on the mesas and plains of Mexico. It is not as important as corn in the daily life of the Mexicans, but *artesanos* long ago discovered the beautiful properties of wheat straw for weaving and plaiting ornamental objects.

The hollow straws of wheat are easily softened in water, and they become very flexible for weaving and braiding. A wet wheat straw can be pinched flat or tied in a knot and it will not break or split.

Hanging wheat straw ornaments made for Christmas are: airy flying birds in three or four sizes, angels of different kinds and stars or sunbursts. Wheat straw miniatures are: straw airplanes, baskets, doll hats, and some flat little animals of very clever woven construction that have a sophisticated stylization about the designs.

Michoacán is know for objects made of wheat straw, and its products are called *panicua*. The village of Tzintzuntzán in Michoacán is noted for straw animal figures, and in Mexico City, craftsmen make small ornamental bird cages out of straw and set tiny wax birds inside.

104

Four small, flat creatures: fish, two elephants (?) and a lion, woven or plaited out of wheat straw—*panicua*—to be used as ornaments or as tiny toys. Height 2½″ to 3½″ (6.4 to 8.9 cm.)

T

Tempera Paints

These inexpensive, opaque colors made with an albuminous base are water-soluble and are used to paint most of the handcrafted objects or toys in Mexico that are not colored with ceramic colors or aniline dyes. This includes toys and small objects of fired unglazed clay, dozens of papier mâché pieces: masks, figures, kites, paper objects, fireworks figures and even sometimes also wooden toys.

Pottery piggy bank of impressive size, painted white and decorated with red, yellow, blue, dark green and gold tempera; made at Tonalá, Jalisco. Height 8¾″, length 9″ (22.2 × 22.9 cm.) *From the collection of Jean and Russell Ames.*

Tin

The Spanish taught Mexicans how to form and mold tin-plate, and at first the work resembled typical Spanish mirror frames, candle sticks, pierced and punched lanterns and other pieces. These are still made and sold as "colonial" tin, and some of it is quite handsome.

But the brightly colored tin Christmas ornaments, boxes and trinkets of present-day Mexico have a flavor that is not Spanish, and they are purchased by many visitors. Most of the ornaments and box parts are cut out by hand with tin snips, following lines scratched on the tin around brass or cardboard patterns—or sometimes absolutely free-hand. The punching and piercing tools are of iron or steel and are usually designed by each individual tin worker, and made for him in a foundry. The punching is done by hammering the tools into a stack of three or four identical pieces of tin against a thick chunk of lead. Pieces of tin are joined together by the use of ordinary lead solder, and two soldering irons are kept hot on a charcoal brazier and used alternately as the artisan works. The soldering is done very skilfully with large, awkward-looking heavy irons.

The Velasco family of tinsmiths in Oaxaca consists of father, mother and a married son who lives next door. The two houses are modest dwellings on a hillside in the outskirts of the city. The Velascos sell their output through the state marketing organization for craftsmen, of which son, Aarón, is an officer. Señora Velasco, a small, quiet woman does most of the designing and soldering, and all of the painting of the tin work. Father and son do the cutting and punching, and Aarón makes some of his own designs. Like all Mexican craftsmen we have spent time with, they are simple, quiet, and very politely cordial people and modest about their work—but they are very much pleased when you admire it. Aarón keeps a neat album of photographs of his work, and of himself at various fairs and events of the organization of artisans.

Serafina Velasco painting aniline colors on an elaborate tin figure of Napoleon, of her design and making. Oaxaca. *Right:* José Velasco punching four layers of tin fastened together with temporary tabs, working with a steel tool on a thick piece of lead. Oaxaca.

Two tin boxes, punched and painted with aniline colors: red, yellow, blue and green. Made by José and Serafina Velasco in Oaxaca City. Round box 2″ in diameter (5.1 cm.) Rectangular box 4⅛″ × 2¼″ × 1⅛″ (10.5 × 5.7 × 2.9 cm.)

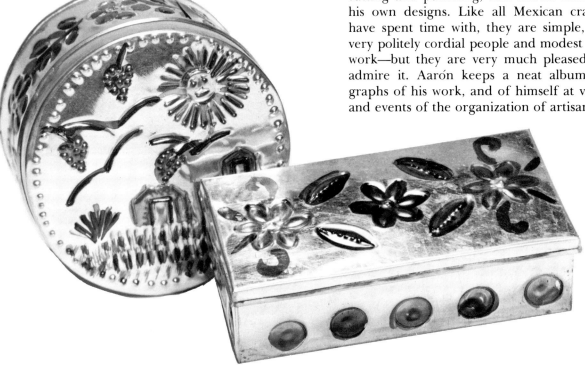

V

Vanilla Beans

Those long, black, wrinkled strips sold in North American markets in glass tubes are dried vanilla beans with which the cook can concoct her own aromatic sweet flavoring for cakes and cookies.

In Mexico, in areas where the vanilla bean grows, and before the bean has dried and turned black, another use is found for it. In Papantla, Vera Cruz, the Totonac Indians grow these beans and pick them in the spring of the year when they are green, smooth and pliant. They weave and twist the fragrant vegetable into strange little creatures: scorpions, lizards, birds and fish as well as flowers and human figures. The natives stage a Vanilla Festival to honor the Indian Vanilla Goddess, and this happens to coincide with the ten-day Corpus Christi festival in June. In Papantla, this is the time of year when one can see the spectacular Flying Pole Dance performed. Vanilla bean figures are also made in Huehuetla, Puebla.

Children love to play with the sweet-smelling toys, and adults use them as pomanders to perfume the air indoors, and, of course, Mexican cooks also use the extract as a flavoring.

Vanilla bean ornament-toys: crucifix and flower form. Height: 1⅝″ and 1½″ (4.1 and 3.8 cm.)

W

Wax

Beeswax was used extensively in Mexico in the eighteenth century as a modeling material to make figures built around a wooden core. *Nacimientos* were made for Christmas with beautifully-sculptured figures of the holy family; sometimes the figures had real hair and beards and were dressed in cloth robes; the clothing was also coated with wax. At the same period there was a vogue for "character" sculptures which were displayed in elegant homes protected by bell-shaped glass covers. There were whole scenes modeled in wax such as bull fights and weddings, and some had other materials and jewels added for realism. The figures were usually about a foot tall (30 cm.) and occupied a place of importance in fashionable parlors. Some of these are to be seen in museums, but they are no longer made.

White dove ornament with papier maché body, pleated paper wings and tail and wax head; feet made of wire covered with red crêpe paper. Length, beak to tail 6¾″ (17.1 cm.)

Two figures: devil and witch with wire springs for arms, legs and necks; cloth garments; heads, hands and feet of painted clay. The devil holds a head on a stick. Height 4¾″ (12.1 cm.)

Beeswax is used today by the Huichol Indians, but only as a mastic to make their bead-lined votive bowls and their *nearikas,* or wool yarn pictures.

Paraffin is used by modern artisans to make the bodies of pairs of two small fighting cocks, each at the end of a long stick—a feathered toy much enjoyed by the two children who stage the fight. Wax is also used to make tiny ornamental bird cages with small wax birds inside; sometimes the cages are made of wheat straw. A popular hanging Christmas ornament is a white papier mâché dove with finely-pleated paper wings and tail and a paraffin head.

One of the very special wax products of Mexico is the wax candles of all sizes that are used on special occasions in the church. These are decorated with hand-formed wax flowers, and may be seen on altars for all special services. Puebla City is know for producing the candles.

Wire Springs

Wire springs are a favorite device of toymakers—especially when used with both small and large papier mâché or clay figures of skeletons for the Day of the Dead. The wiggly arms and legs and the bobbing heads attached to bodies by springy necks are evidently thought to be very scary. They are also used for making devils, witches, spiders and Judas animals.

Wood

The two most-used materials for the handcrafts of Mexico are probably clay and thread or yarn for weaving. But for the making of *toys,* wood is surely the indispensable and irreplaceable stuff of the craft. There is even a unique plywood less than one-eighth of an inch thick (3 cm.) manufactured in sheets especially for toymaking in Mexico. It is called *tejamanil,* which really means *shingle,* but is translated as "scrap wood." But this is not a discarded scrap, as the translation might indicate. The wood itself is probably pine, or a similar soft wood—the same as that used in other pieces of all sizes for making toys.

In Oaxaca, in the house of the man who made the ferris wheel (See color plate.) one boy and two little girls about 11, 9 and 7 years old are kept busy in the tiny workroom, sandpapering thin strips of wood for their father to use to build the two sizes of his specialty, the *Rueda de Fortuna,* or wheel of fortune

Manuel Jiménez, wood carver, with his son Angelo who is learning his father's trade. They are holding unpainted copal wood carvings—some of the *nacimiento* figures for which Jiménez is famous. Arrasola, Oaxaca, 1976.

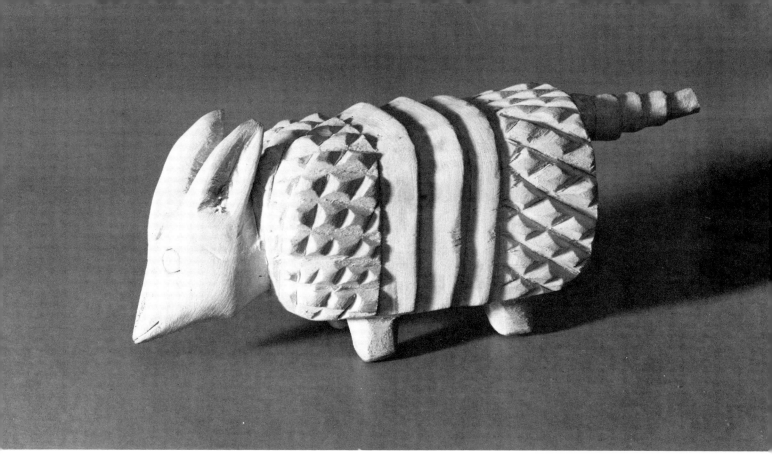

Armadillo, carved of unpainted copal wood by a farmer-adobe brick maker known only as *Gordo* (Fatty) in San Martin Tilcajete, Oaxaca. Height 2⅛″ (5.4 cm.)

with its riders. The wood pieces are put together with wire, glue and small nails and are painted with bright aniline colors. The workers and the method are typical of Mexican toy-making establishments.

The many charming and often primitive hand-carved animals, *nacimiento* figures, small churches, etc. seen in Mexico are often made of *copal* or *copalillo*—a white, even-grained wood from a tree that grows all over the country. Not only the wood of this tree is serviceable, but the gum is used to make most of the ceremonial incense used in Mexico. The wood is very moist when freshly cut, and is comparatively easy to carve. Most carvers use exactly three tools, from tree to finished product: a *machete*, a knife and a chisel, nothing more. Sometimes the carvings are smoothed with sandpaper, more often not. As the wood dries it shrinks and gets harder, thus a pair of ears stuck into two holes dug out of a wooden coyote's head will tighten up and fit more securely when dry than if they were glued. There is no mystery about how legs and tails are fastened to bodies—one or two plainly-seen black-headed nails do the job. Most of the details of faces, hands, claws, etc. are painted, not carved. Many of the animals have a primitive and amusing look about them that is most endearing. The

work of less skilled carvers and of imitators seems to lack the subtle animation of the more appealing pieces. Some of the carvings, whether painted or not may seem to be sculpture rather than toys. But one of the internationally-known craftsmen of Mexico, wood carver Manuel Jiménez of Arrasola, Oaxaca, became very upset when we suggested that his work should be called sculpture. "¡*No*, señora, *no soy escultor;* mis obras son juguetes, *juguetes!*" "*No,* I am not a sculptor—my work is toys, *toys.*" So be it, then—toys for all ages.

A list of the wooden playthings of Mexico is almost endless, and a new toy may be discovered in every village. There are carved animals, people, birds, jointed snakes, tops, cup-and-ball, push-toys, pull-toys, matracas, jumping jacks, acrobats on a ladder, *nacimiento* figures, boxers, frameworks for *castillos,* kites and fireworks toys, doll houses, doll furniture, dozens of miniatures, toy musical instruments, reed flutes, guns, swords and carved models for making molds for *alfeñique* confections, lead soldiers, papier maché toys and pottery toys.

109

A word of warning to purchasers of any wood carvings in Mexico: when you get home, if you find tiny piles of white dust under a carving after a few days, you will know that live worms are at work. Put each carving or toy, or several small ones together, in a tightly-closed plastic bag with a few moth balls, and leave it for a week or more. This will kill the worms that are eating their way into your wood carvings.

Summary

The list tells us clearly that the toymaker of Mexico makes use of any material that may be at hand, and that he also seeks and finds materials of unexpected kinds and puts them to ingenious uses.

It is doubtful that any other country could cite toys and decorations made from as many materials as those listed above—and there are even more. But the distinctive quality of the objects on this list is that they are almost entirely *made by hand*. Such pieces could not possibly come from machines or a factory assembly line. Since this is true of most of the toys and other folkcrafts of the country, it must be agreed that their charm, color and variety come from the inventive and somehow rather innocent minds and skilled hands of hundreds of Mexican artisans.

Wood carver *Gordo* (Fatty) at work on one of his unpainted copal wood animals. *Gordo* is a farmer and an adobe brick maker at San Martin Tilcajete, Oaxaca.

"Gordo" the toymaker's son with a toy he improvised from an old wheel and a reed stick.

110

V

A CALENDAR OF TRADITIONAL MEXICAN HOLIDAYS, FESTIVALS AND FIESTAS

Above: Mask, "Cat"—papier maché, mold-pressed, painted pink, gold, black and white, Made in Celaya, Guanajuato. Width 7½″, height 7″ (19.1 × 17.8 cm.)

IN MEXICO, occasions worth noting occur every month of the year, and Mexicans young and old are always ready and eager for a celebration. Some towns have as many as thirty festivals of one kind or another during one year. Some of the most impressive pageants, folkloric dances, fiestas and processions take place in only one village of the country, and a visitor would have to travel fast and far to see them all. Many festivals are held to commemorate dates and heroes of Mexican history, and, of course, in honor of the saints or holy days of the Catholic church; but in remote areas of Mexico, the celebrations honor the pagan gods that still govern the lives of many Indians. In some cases celebrations are a mixture of Christian and pagan influences and are interesting because of the combination. Fiestas, which are not necessarily religious celebrations, often take place at the end of a holy occasion, and sometimes they are an entirely separate and joyful festivity of their own.

Octavio Paz says of fiestas: "This is the night when friends who have not exchanged more than the prescribed courtesies for months get drunk together, trade confidences, weep over the same troubles, discover they are brothers, and sometimes to prove it, kill each other. The night is full of sounds and loud cries. The lover wakes up his sweetheart with an orchestra. There are jokes from balcony to balcony, sidewalk to sidewalk. Nobody talks quietly. Hats fly in the air. Laughter and curses ring like silver pesos. Guitars are brought out. Mexico is celebrating a fiesta."*

The most holy and solemn observances, as well as the fiestas sometimes begin and often end with the favorite celebration of all Mexicans—fireworks—*fuegos artificiales.* The *alborada,* reveille, explosions start at about 5 A.M. to signal the first mass or the beginning of a fiesta everywhere, even in the smallest and poorest villages, and the

*Paz, *The Labyrinth of Solitude,* p. 49.

111

sporadic noise does not stop until after midnight. If a fiesta starts on Sunday afternoon it is often begun with a bullfight, then climaxed by fireworks. Churches and towns pay a considerable sum to the local professional *pirotécnico* to construct and shoot off a variety of spectacular fireworks, especially that masterpiece of explosive color—the *castillo,* or castle.

Many toys are an important part of Mexican festivals. The principal religious festivals are Christmas (December 25), Festival of the Virgin of Guadalupe (December 12) and Holy Week and Easter in the spring. Others with important religious overtones, but with distinctive characteristics of their own are Day of the Dead (November 2), Corpus Christi (June) and the Day of the Three Kings (January 6.) Independence Day has been celebrated on September 15 since the 1910 revolution, and is a national holiday. In addition to all these, there are scores of other religious celebrations, unique village festivals, fiestas and Indian rituals.

Some of the traditional toys and decorative objects of Mexico that are not a part of specific festivals, but seem to belong to them all are: cutout paper street banners, flower-decorated wax candles, masks and dozens upon dozens of miniature playthings. Some of these cannot be called toys, or decorations, or sculpture, but a little of all three, and they are all distinctively Mexican.

Villages decorated with *papel picado*—the fluttery little cut-paper flags and banners—lend a festive air to the whole town. The women and girls of the village cut out the tissue paper and hang the decorations up themselves. Some occasions, such as Corpus Christi Day in June and the Day of the Dead in November have special Mexican connotations and there are objects and decorations appearing at those times that do not exist at any other time. In short, Mexicans celebrate everything in a joyful style that is reflected in their decorations and toys as well as in their passionate love for the tumult and color of fireworks.

Little girl street vendor selling giant balloons, Mexico City, New Year's Day, 1976.

Fancy paper and plastic hats for New Year's and Three
Kings Day, Mexico City, January 1, 1976.

THE YEAR'S EVENTS

JANUARY

1

New Year's Eve is not the animated occasion
that might be expected in Mexico, but is celebrated
at dinners and supper parties in a rather quiet way.
It is a time when crowds of Mexican families dressed
in their best stroll the streets until after midnight,
and street vendors are kept busy selling balloons,
trinkets and food of all kinds. Church services on
New Year's day are well attended, as Mexico marks
the end of one year and the beginning of another.

6

January 6 is Epiphany—a feast of the Catholic
church which commemorates the coming of the
Magi, as the first manifestation of Christ to the
Gentiles. In Mexico, and in most Latin-American
countries, January 6 is the day of the year that
children anticipate with the greatest excitement—
because it is the Day of the Three Kings—*el día de
los Reyes* (or *Santos Reyes*) the day they receive their
annual gifts. In that one respect it is, in European
and North American terms, their Christmas Day.
Christmas, on the other hand, is not a time for
giving and receiving gifts, but is a holy day reserved
for worship honoring the birth of Christ. As the
Magi brought gifts to the Christ Child in

Children posing with the Three Kings in Alameda Park, Mexico City on January 6th. The children are riding papier maché animals: a horse, a camel and an elephant; the black King, Balthazar stands in the center of the picture.

Bethlehem twelve days after His birth, so they are believed to bring gifts on Epiphany and leave them in the shoes of Mexican children each year on the 6th of January. (See color plate).

On Epiphany it is customary to serve a fancy cake decorated with fruit called *Rosca de Reyes*—"twisted cake of the Kings." It contains a tiny porcelain figure of the Christ Child, and whoever receives this has to give a party on February second—*día de la Candelaría.*

The three Kings of the Bible are very important figures in Christmas season pageants in Mexico and they appear "in person" in parks and plazas, especially in the Alameda Park in Mexico City. They are tall men in theatrical makeup and false beards, wearing resplendent robes and gold crowns. Children wait in line to have their pictures taken by the sidewalk photographers with the awesome kings.

Toys sold by street vendors in the cities in January include small crowns, fancy hats and headdresses, masks with fierce mustaches and some all-black masks representing Balthazar, the black King, along with dozens of conventional toys such as balloons, pinwheels, puppets and mechanical toys. The small masks representing the Kings are made of papier mâché painted in bright colors, and are a modern-day toy derived from the masks that have been used for years in Mexican rituals, dances and pageants.

15

A colorful fiesta is staged in the dusty little weaving village of Teotitlan del Valle, Oaxaca, on January 15th and is an opportunity to see the famous traditional Indian Feather Dancers in action.

17

January 17th is St. Anthony's Day—when children take their pets or farm animals to the church to be blessed by the priest. This is a charming ceremony to see.

20

For a week beginning January 20 there are fiestas in both Mitla and San Pablo, Oaxaca, featuring Feather Dancers, and there are fiestas from January 20th to 25th in Tehuantepec, Oaxaca.

Street photographer's painted velvet background in Alameda Park on January 6th. The religious painting is surrounded by paper flowers, angels, saints, balloons, toys and plastic poinsettias.

FEBRUARY

2

February 2nd is Candelmas Day when candles are lighted to honor the infant Jesus. His figure is taken out of the Christmas *nacimiento* and dressed in new clothes. Many parties are given on this date which marks the end of all Christmas festivities.

8

From the 2nd of the month to the 8th of February celebrations continue in honor of the Virgin of La Candelaría. There are fiestas, bullfights, processions and ceremonies to bless seeds and candles. The occasions are marked in an especially colorful way at Teotihuacán near Mexico City, at Tlacotalpan, Vera Cruz and at the village of Tzintzuntzan in Michoacán.

24

Flag Day is a national holiday marked by parades on February 24th.

25

Between February 25 and March 5 there are carnivals and celebrations all over Mexico during which there are Indian dances, costume parades, pageants and fiestas of all sorts. *Carnaval* time is traditionally a last fling before Ash Wednesday when the solemnity and fasting of Lent begin. There are especially gay carnivals at Campeche, Tampico, Mazatlan and Vera Cruz. Masks are worn by many of the festival participants to identify characters in a pageant, to serve as disguises, or to provide a way for simple village and country people to assume a temporarily changed personality.

Giant carnival figures with papier maché heads, always seen at village fiestas; el Alhondiga Museum, Guanajuato City.

Masks in the museum el Alhondiga at Guanajuato City.

115

MARCH

1

On the first of this month one of the oldest Mexican festivals is held in the city of Durango—an impressive fiesta and fair in honor of "The Soldiers' Christ."

The carnivals of late February continue to March 5, by which date Lent has often begun—the date varies from year to year.

4

On March 4 there is a religious festival in the beautiful colonial town of Taxco, in Guerrero. There are pastoral plays performed by young people dressed as cocks in bright costumes, and this is of particular interest to children.

9

A week-long fiesta of local Indians is held in Etla, Oaxaca, with processions honoring a local image, "The Lord of Sorrows". This tiny village, otherwise a very quiet one, is crowded with country people who come to participate solemnly in this celebration that begins on March 9th.

Woodcut by Roberto Montenegro, illustrating an article titled "The Carnival of Zaachila, Oaxaca" by Rafael and Monna Sala.

18

A one-day market at Tepaltzingo, Morelia takes place at which primitive pottery animals produced locally are sold, on March 18th.

19

On March 19th the feast of San José is celebrated everywhere in Mexico. All boys and men name José (and there are a lot), all the churches of San José and all the villages of that name enjoy a festive celebration in honor of their patron, St. Joseph.

Perhaps the largest fiesta of the pre-Lenten season (on a movable date in March) in Mexico is the one at Huejotzingo, Puebla—a tiny village that is transformed by the arrival of throngs of hundreds of masked, costumed participants representing characters in the story they are reenacting. These are: the Empress Carlotta—who is kidnapped from her carriage as the action proceeeds—French Zoaves, Apaches, Hungarians, Turks and colonial Indians. The day-long pageant is enacted with realistic battles, and ends with the hero being "shot" by French Zoaves, as he was in real life. The pageant is notable because it is not of Spanish, Catholic or pagan origin, but honors a native Indian hero named Augustín Lorenzo, a local much-admired outlaw of colonial days who robbed the rich Spaniards and gave to the poor Indians.

21

Mexico celebrates a national holiday on March 21, birthday of Benito Juárez, the Zapotec Indian who became a great leader in the 1850's, and is considered to be the first statesman of the country who advocated modern reforms in the government of his country.

MARCH—APRIL

On the Tuesday before Ash Wednesday when Lent begins there is a different sort of all-day carnival at Zaachila, Oaxaca in which masqueraders are divided into two groups—devils and priests. The red, green or multi-color-clad devils spend the day chasing and bedeviling the priests who are dressed in black and white. The crowds that have gathered to eat and drink in a festive mood often join in the antics and pursuits.

The period of Lent, culminating on Easter Sunday is celebrated throughout Catholic Mexico to commemorate the crucifixion and resurrection of Christ. The Mexican converts to Catholicism in the seventeenth and eighteenth centuries learned the new religion very thoroughly, and now, all over Mexico until Palm Sunday there is an impressive medley of sound from solemn church bells everywhere to announce services and holy days. The Spanish also introduced fireworks into Mexico, so you will often hear firecrackers being shot off to announce the first mass on the same holy days. The Mexican has a gift for finding his own way of expressing his feelings on important occasions—and his expression is apt to be ebullient.

There are still colorful pagan elements in some pre-Easter festivals and in Indian villages there are celebrations during this period that have their origins in the rites of spring performed long ago.

On Friday before Palm Sunday a beautiful church holiday decoration is arranged, especially in the churches of Puebla and Morelos. It is called the "Altar of Sorrows" and it is decorated with cut-paper banners, paper and real flowers, ornamented wax candles, miniature pots of flowers and blown-glass globes filled with colored water. In the plaza outside the same churches a carpet of flowers is laid down in colorful designs.

Holy Week

Mexican children are very fond of a yellowish, sweet taffy called *charamusca* which is pulled and shaped into dolls, animals and other forms and is sold in markets. During Holy Week, candy "crowns of thorns" are made of this plastic, sticky stuff—chiefly in Celaya and Michoacán. The candy crown of thorns may be called the more religious counterpart of the American chocolate Easter egg.

The week before Easter is observed in Christian churches as Holy Week (*Semana Santa*), and it begins on Palm Sunday. The celebration of this week is said to have originated in Seville, Spain, but now it has taken on a Mexican character.

Palm Sunday is a very important occasion in the Catholic church. The use of palm leaves is a custom based on the story that when Jesus arrived in Jerusalem his followers waved palm leaves and olive branches to greet him and to express their devotion. In Mexico, where palm trees are native to the warmer regions, the leaves are used to make beautiful symbols of that ceremony which began so long ago.

Palm leaf sun ornament to be carried to church on Palm Sunday; natural color. Made in Guadalajara, Jalisco. Height 15″, diameter 11⅝″ (38.1 × 29.5 cm.)

Palm leaf flowers, made for Palm Sunday; natural and colored magenta and green. Height 6¼″ (15.9 cm.)

Palm ornament to be carried on Palm Sunday; an exquisitely stylized construction made of natural palm leaf. Made in Guadalajara, Jalisco. L 20″ (50.8 cm.)

In cities where there is a large church, and especially if there is a cathedral, the native artisans living nearby quietly gather on the church plaza the night before Palm Sunday, and spend the night there. They bring with them a supply of the young heart leaves of the palm tree, and very early Sunday morning they arise and begin to weave and plait their intricate and decorative designs made of the soft green leaves. Even in small villages there are artisans who are skilled in making these lovely *palmas* for their own village churches.

Before the first mass begins, people come to look at the array of finished palm ornaments and bargain for the prettiest ones to carry into the church on this very holy day. Each member of the family carries a palm leaf of some kind, and each is blessed by the priest with holy water and a prayer; the leaves are held in the hands of the members of the congregation during the service.

Afterward, the people take their *palmas* home and give them a place on the wall or over a doorway as a holy symbol to remain in place all year. It is said that during storms a few of the palm leaves are ceremonially burned to protect the home from lightening. This is a rather charming example of Indian superstition that is inextricably woven into Christian reverence.

On Ash Wednesday of the following year, by which time the *palmas* have long since dried to a pale gold color, the same leaves are taken to the church again to be burned and the ashes are used by the priest to make the mark of the cross on the foreheads of worshippers at the beginning of a new Easter season.

Holy Week sees some of the most solemn and impressive celebrations of the year in Mexico. There are religious plays, processions, church services and fiestas as well as a few other uniquely Mexican happenings. Some villages that are of special interest during the celebration of Holy Week are San Miguel de Allende, Ixtapalapa, Tzintzuntzán and Taxco. In the latter town there is a religious procession of black-hooded *penitentes,* sometimes walking on their knees, bearing thorn branches and shedding their blood as Christ shed His when crowned with thorns. Village participants carry statues of Christ and the Virgin and the procession ends at Santa Prisca church where there is an impressive service. Passion Plays dramatizing the Last Supper and the Crucifixion are soberly enacted in many towns by costumed villagers and are charming, traditional folk plays that are completely absorbing to both young and old audiences.

Palm frond woven into a decorative ornament to be carried into the church on Palm Sunday. Made in Guadalajara, Jalisco. Length 30″ (76.2 cm.)

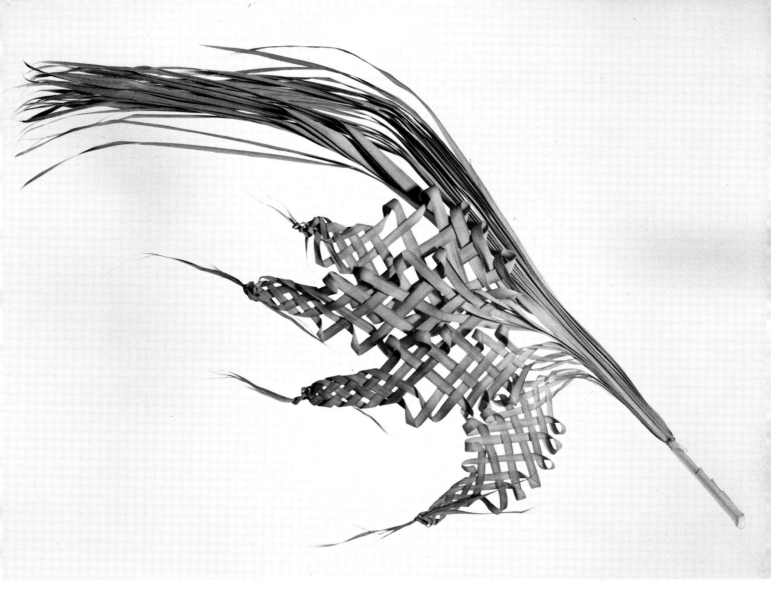

Palm frond woven into a decorative form, to be carried on Palm Sunday; natural color. Made in Guadalajara, Jalisco. Length 27″ (68.6 cm.)

Palm frond woven into a simple design that manages to seem to be an improvement on nature; natural color. Made in Guadalajara, Jalisco. Length 27″ (68.6 cm.)

119

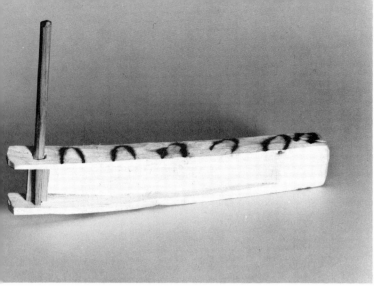

Matraca, noise-maker made of unpainted wood, decorated primitively with a burned design; the two edge pieces and the thin, noisemaking blade in the center are carved out of one piece, and the noise it makes is fearsome. Handle is 5½″ long, the blade 9¼″ (14 × 23.5 cm.)

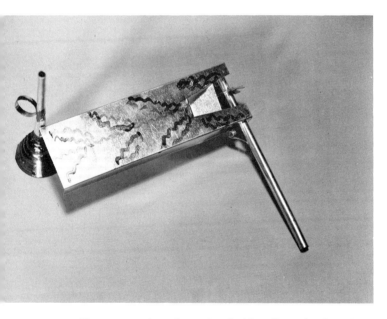

Tin *matraca* noisemaker, painted with aniline colors in red and blue; an all-purpose celebration toy, since it whirrs when swung, and attached to one end is a tin horn that gives a good blast when blown. Handle 6″ long, blade 6″ long (15.2 cm.)

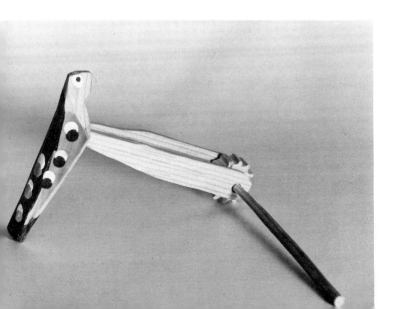

Metal cut by José Guadalupe Posada from a novel. The illustration is titled "*La Matraca.*"

During Holy Week, until Easter, church bells are silenced in Mexico, and masses are heralded by the staccato sound of noisemakers called *matracas.* In the United States this whirling gadget with a toothed wheel that chatters against the edge of a thin piece of wood is sometimes used by celebrants on New Year's Eve or Hallowe'en. But large ones serve a more or less religious purpose in Mexico. The *matracas* may also be made of tin and both kinds are noisily swung in toy size around the heads of children everywhere in Mexico at Easter time. In colonial days delicate silver *matracas* were made by silversmiths and these were decorated with tiny horses, birds, flowers and costumed figures. They could be purchased in jewelry stores for elegant Easter gifts. The silver *matracas* are now rare museum pieces.

Resurrection Day

From colonial days up to very recent years a unique ceremony was enacted in Mexico on Holy Saturday. The day before Easter was marked by the destruction of huge papier mâché figures representing Judas, the betrayer of Christ. In April, 1977, not one large Judas could be discovered in Mexico City. It is possible that the event still takes place in neigh-

Wood matraca noisemaker toy with painted bird. Length 5½″ (14 cm.)

borhood plazas, or in other cities, but we can only mourn the passing of this colorful celebration in Mexico's capitol city.

The celebration is based on a Spanish custom, but it gradually took on a distinctly Mexican style. On Maundy Thursday and Good Friday there began to appear on the streets large papier mâché and bamboo constructions that represented Judas, and the effigies embodied all the nefarious characters known in Mexico. The figures ranged in size from doll-sized papier mâché animals, devils and clowns to towering forms twelve feet tall.

The smaller toy Judases are still made at Easter time and can be bought for a few pesos in some markets and shops, and from street vendors. They are rather crudely made and are painted in bright tempera colors, but they serve well as special toys for the season. Judases, large or small, take the form of animals, horned devils, unpopular historical figures, bandits, caricatures of disliked local officials, or simply weird, comic or ugly men. (See color plate) None of them ever resembles a Biblical figure. Diego Rivera painted two portraits of a little girl holding a Judas horse, and one of his frescoes in the Ministry of Education Building in Mexico City pictures the Judases as "The Bourgeois Politician, the General on Horseback and the Priest" shown in front of a large crowd of people.

The very large Judases used to be hung up in public plazas or set up in parks and outside of stores in certain streets where shopkeepers hung sweets or bits of bread on the figures. Sometimes thirty pieces of "silver" were sewn to the clothes of Judas to identify him as the traitor.

The important thing about the giant figures is that they were completely strung with explosive fireworks. On Saturday after the Mass of Glory, the crowds gathered around, the fuse was lighted and the Judas slowly and noisily blew to bits, to the accompaniment of much shouting. This was a typically Mexican interpretation of the symbolic act of punishing Judas and of destroying evil. The children scrambled for the blown-off candies, relishing the noise, smoke, confusion and the rewards. Diego Rivera said of the Judases: ". . . these are works of art intended to be sacrificed for the merriment and the fierce enjoyment of the country that produces them. They have, then, a marvelous destiny."*

Judas, who suffered such a devastating demise was perhaps the clearest example of the Mexican attitude toward toys that are cheaply made and not expected to last long, as well as toward colorful

*Rivera and Wolfe, *Portrait of Mexico.*

121

Judas doll—devil with horns and wings; papier mâché painted with tempera colors: purple body with white, black, pink and blue details. Height 17″ (43.2 cm.)

Judas doll with sombrero; papier mâché painted with tempera colors—white with red decoration, pink face and blue hat. Made in Guanajuato City. Height 11″ (27.9 cm.)

Giant Judas with sombrero, wired with explosives; painted papier maché. Height 12 feet (3.66 m.)

Giant Judas, skeleton; painted papier maché. Height 12 feet (3.66 m.)

Giant Judas, gentleman in top hat, wired with explosives, painted papier maché. Height 12 feet (3.66 m.)

Giant Judas, clown wired with explosives; painted papier maché. Height 12 feet (3.66 m.)

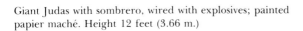

decorations for all special occasions. No amount of work and skilled artistry are too much, and no expense is too great to produce the colorful accoutrements of an important event. The fact that gimcrack toys, wax candles, flowers, *piñatas* and *castillos* do not last very long does not matter at all—if they are pretty, appropriate and important to the occasion. The artisans who used to spend long hours making the huge Judases and those who still make the fireworks *castillo* and other small figures are more ecstatic than any of the other observers during their fiery display and explosive destruction. Many solemn Mexican ceremonies are followed by a jubilant celebration of some kind. In the past the Easter Mass of Glory was not properly complete until Judas had met his end. It is a pity that the ceremony is no longer enacted in most places.

There was a rather obscure Spanish custom from which the Judas may have been derived. The noisy Mexican event seems to have had no religious connotation originally, but stemmed from a Spanish festival held during Lent called *Partir de la Vieja*—departure (or death) of the Old Woman—perhaps winter. A grotesque figure was kept hanging in public view until Holy Saturday when it was drowned in the sea so as to destroy it forever. In some seaport towns of Spain there is still a figure that is drowned called *El Pelele,* the Scarecrow.

Spring visitors to Mexico will see Mexico's famous churches at their resplendent best for Easter services—a beautiful setting for the triumphant and joyous celebration of the Resurrection.

Giant Judas, figure with a big-eared animal head; painted papier maché. Height 12 feet (3.66 m.)

Giant Judas, grinning horned devil with devil heads on elbows and knees and a snake-entwined torso; painted papier maché. Height 12 feet (3.66 m.)

APRIL

A gay, annual market day fiesta in Etla, Oaxaca with Indian folk dances takes place on the first day of April.

The first week in April, the town of San Cristóbal de las Casas in Chiapas celebrates its founding. This is the oldest colonial city in the state and one of the most charming in Mexico.

From April 25th to May 5th one of Mexico's largest and most colorful fiestas, called the San Marco Fair, takes place at Aguascalientes City; and there are many local village fiestas in this post-Lenten season.

123

Churchyard cross, Santo Tomás Jalieza, Oaxaca.

MAY

1

Mexico's Labor Day is May 1, and it is a national holiday celebrated everywhere with miles of parades.

3

On May 3rd the country celebrates the feast of the Holy Cross—on the date that was once considered by the Mayans of Yucatán to be the most auspicious for spring planting. Now, homage is paid to the cross in its many forms as the symbol of Christianity. Crosses at roadside shrines and in villages are decorated with flowers, and all miraculous crosses are especially honored and thanked. There are many village fiestas on this date.

In larger cities May 3rd has somehow become the day when all builders, brick layers, masons, carpenters and construction workers pay homage to their trade. The only discernible connection between this group and the Day of the Holy Cross seems to be that it is customary to set up crosses made of reed or cane at the topmost point of all new buildings, and on this day all buildings under construction are topped with crosses laden with flowers. It has been said that May 3rd is an "all-out, nation-wide bomb-burst," and when the explosions start, all connection with the cross appears to end. If Mexicans are content with firecrackers and rockets to celebrate other occasions, for this day they require cannon crackers and aerial bombs! All construction work stops at noon; the bombardment begins, and the merry-making, drinking and noise are still going on past midnight. It is a day when other citizens have no choice but to be indulgent about the warlike racket made by the liberated builders.

5

On May 5th there is a Mexican national holiday which commemorates the 1863 Battle of Puebla, when the French invaded Mexico and declared the country a monarchy.

15

Mexico celebrates *El día de San Isidro,* patron saint of rain and farming on May 15th. Farm animals are decorated with flowers and ribbons and brought into villages to be blessed by the priests.

An evening fiesta with dancing follows the ceremonies.

JUNE

1

Between the end of May and the 15th of June, Mexico celebrates Corpus Christi Day; this is a so-called movable feast, and the date changes from year to year. It is essentially a religious day that originated in festivals honoring the eucharist of the Catholic church. Annual festivals in many villages celebrate this occasion with services followed by a great variety of fiestas.

In colonial days the plaza of the Cathedral in Mexico City was thronged on Corpus Christi Day with children costumed in village Indian dress. The boys had small wooden crates filled with fruits and flowers tied to their backs. All the children attended a special service in the Cathedral; village churches followed the same custom. The custom originated in the fact that many years ago mule trains carrying the earliest fruits and other goods arrived in Mexico City from the port of Acapulco early in June, and were blessed upon their arrival in the *zócalo*. It is still the custom today for children to assemble and carry the "first fruits" to the church to be blessed by a priest.

A traditional Corpus Christi toy has survived in the form of a little mule, or *mulito* made of corn stalks and corn husks or banana leaves, painted with a few bright splashes of color. Its load is a pair of small wooden crates of sweets decorated with flowers; the toy is made in many sizes from tiny straw or palm leaf miniatures to those of twelve inches in height. Probably every young child is given (or used to be given) a *mulito* on Corpus Christi, but the decorative little animals are almost impossible to find at any other time of the year. Unfortunately the handmade *mulitos* appear to be in danger of disappearing completely. (See color plate)

Villages celebrate this holiday in their own unique way. At Papantla, Vera Cruz the Flying Pole Dance is performed as part of its fiesta, and this attracts visitors from far and wide. In other areas mock markets are held in which all the goods are made in miniature and are given to children after a pretended bargaining and an exchange of bogus money. But everywhere there are fiestas with music and dancing on Corpus Christi.

Palm leaf *mulitos*—a traditional Corpus Christi toy; natural color with touches of red and green dye. Small, 1¼″ tall, medium, 3¼″ (3.2 and 8.3 cm.)

Little girl in Indian dress carrying a basket of "first fruits" to the church to be blessed on Corpus Christi Day in June.

Above and opposite page: Pink and yellow cut tissue paper banners, strung up as decorations on all festive occasions. 17″ × 13″ (43.2 × 33 cm.)

24

June 24 is the feast day of St. John the Baptist, which is first celebrated at church services, then some villagers join in communal bathing wherever there are nearby rivers and streams. A colonial custom of this date has almost entirely disappeared—the costumed battle of the Moors and Christians fought by young boys. Special accessories and toys were made for the children—spears, swords, daggers and paper-headed horses on sticks. Small turbans, hats, robes and coats were worn by participants fighting the mock battle to the cry of "Moor or Christian?" Paper horses and a few toy swords may still appear in markets, but the battle is now seldom reenacted. There is, however, a masked folk dance based on this tradition called *Los Moros* performed in Michoacán, Papantla, Iguala and elsewhere on June 24.

JULY

6

Indians in native costume gather to stage a unique hilltop ceremony to make offerings of hair and personal belongings on July 6th in Tlacotepec, Puebla.

8

In the village of Teotitlan del Valle in Oaxaca, practically every house is the workshop of one of the famous Oaxaca weavers, and a visit to the town is worthwhile just to see the weavers at work making woolen rugs, serapes and hangings. On July 8th every year the normally quiet square of the village is the scene of a fiesta where the colorful Feather Dances are performed.

16

This is a date celebrated all over Mexico on the occasion of the *Fiesta de la Virgen del Carmen.* It is a colorful festival held on July 16th, and it is especially well worth seeing at Oaxaca City, Ciudad del Carmen in Campeche and at Coyoacan.

Band made up of a father and four sons, ages 6 to 14 playing for a village fiesta at San Miguel de Allende.

18

The death of Benito Juarez on July 18th, 1872 is commemorated as a national holiday to honor the father of the Mexican constitution.

AUGUST

15

This is a month of many village festivals and celebrations; the only one that is not entirely local occurs at various locations on August 15th, and is called the Feast of the Assumption.

31

The whole state of Oaxaca celebrates the feast of *San Ramón* on the last day of August; it is a day when priests bless animals of all kinds.

SEPTEMBER

In Mexico City the Mexican Tourist Department stages a festival with music and dancing in Chapultepec Park all during the month of September.

15

September 15th and 16th are marked as the two-day national Independence Day holiday. In describing the Mexicans' enjoyment of a holiday celebration, Octavio Paz says of this one: "Each year on the 15th of September at 11 o'clock at night we celebrate the Fiesta of *El Grito,* the Cry—Padre Hidalgo's call to arms against Spain in 1810—in all the plazas of the Republic, and the excited crowds actually shout for a whole hour . . . the better, perhaps, to remain silent for the rest of the year."*

OCTOBER

12

There are local fiestas in various locations in October, but only one national holiday—*el día de la Raza*—observed on the 12th of the month to commemorate the discovery of America.

*Paz, *The Labyrinth of Solitude,* p. 47.

127

Young Indian boy dancer.

Bread for the Day of the Dead (*pan de muertos*); the forms on top represent a skull in the center, surrounded by bones, all topped with sugar. Diameter 9½″ (24.1 cm.)

Pottery incense burner used on the Day of the Dead; made of fired red clay decorated with dark blue and white tempera paint. The figures around the rim represent souls of the dead. Made in Ocotlán, Oaxaca. Height 3⅞″, diameter 3¾″ (9.8 × 9.5 cm.)

2

This month opens with the most important two-day Indian religious occasion in Mexico, and it is a national holiday. November first is All Saints' Day and the second is All Soul's Day, or the Day of the Dead. These days honor the dead—first, *los angelitos,* little angels, or the children who have died, and the second day of November honors all other dead persons.

On both days it has been believed for years by many Mexicans that the souls of dead persons return to their families for a night's visit, and upon the occasion of this annual reunion of loved ones, the spirits are received and welcomed as honored guests. This traditional belief is still held by many Indians and country people, but Day of the Dead ceremonies are less and less often practiced in Mexico's larger and more modern cities. Many special objects and decorations are still made to celebrate this festival, the most impressive of which is the *ofrenda,* or offering, a beautifully-decorated altar or shrine bearing food, fruit and flowers, paper ornaments, colored glass globes, incense and a candle for each soul. These elaborate altars are set up in many churches and homes, outside cemeteries, and even in humble Indian dwellings a small *ofrenda* is arranged with flowers and candles. Food that was a favorite of certain dead persons is prepared and placed on the altar, sometimes in small baskets or specially-made bowls, and decorated with flowers. Village potters in Oaxaca and elsewhere make special ceremonial incense burners for this occasion, in which fragrant copal incense is burned. Some of them are of pre-Hispanic origin in the form of a shallow, red clay bowl that stands on three legs and has small, white amorphous figures representing souls sitting around the edge. If an altar is dedicated to a child it will hold sweets and toys for the returning soul of the young person.

It is an ancient belief that the dead partake of food in spirit on this night—the only time of the year when they can eat. Afterward, the food is enjoyed by the families in a festive mood because they are happy to have shared it with the souls of their loved and honored relatives. Toys from the offering are later given to other children of the family, or to friends. The sharing of food is so important a part of the Day of the Dead that people hang baskets of food outside their doors so that passing spiritis can partake of it, in case they have no family or friends to feed them. The souls can then return to their graves, reassured that they have not been forgotten.

An evening fiesta with dancing follows the ceremonies.

JUNE
1

Between the end of May and the 15th of June, Mexico celebrates Corpus Christi Day; this is a so-called movable feast, and the date changes from year to year. It is essentially a religious day that originated in festivals honoring the eucharist of the Catholic church. Annual festivals in many villages celebrate this occasion with services followed by a great variety of fiestas.

In colonial days the plaza of the Cathedral in Mexico City was thronged on Corpus Christi Day with children costumed in village Indian dress. The boys had small wooden crates filled with fruits and flowers tied to their backs. All the children attended a special service in the Cathedral; village churches followed the same custom. The custom originated in the fact that many years ago mule trains carrying the earliest fruits and other goods arrived in Mexico City from the port of Acapulco early in June, and were blessed upon their arrival in the *zócalo*. It is still the custom today for children to assemble and carry the "first fruits" to the church to be blessed by a priest.

A traditional Corpus Christi toy has survived in the form of a little mule, or *mulito* made of corn stalks and corn husks or banana leaves, painted with a few bright splashes of color. Its load is a pair of small wooden crates of sweets decorated with flowers; the toy is made in many sizes from tiny straw or palm leaf miniatures to those of twelve inches in height. Probably every young child is given (or used to be given) a *mulito* on Corpus Christi, but the decorative little animals are almost impossible to find at any other time of the year. Unfortunately the handmade *mulitos* appear to be in danger of disappearing completely. (See color plate)

Villages celebrate this holiday in their own unique way. At Papantla, Vera Cruz the Flying Pole Dance is performed as part of its fiesta, and this attracts visitors from far and wide. In other areas mock markets are held in which all the goods are made in miniature and are given to children after a pretended bargaining and an exchange of bogus money. But everywhere there are fiestas with music and dancing on Corpus Christi.

Palm leaf *mulitos*—a traditional Corpus Christi toy; natural color with touches of red and green dye. Small, 1¼″ tall, medium, 3¼″ (3.2 and 8.3 cm.)

Little girl in Indian dress carrying a basket of "first fruits" to the church to be blessed on Corpus Christi Day in June.

24

June 24 is the feast day of St. John the Baptist, which is first celebrated at church services, then some villagers join in communal bathing wherever there are nearby rivers and streams. A colonial custom of this date has almost entirely disappeared—the costumed battle of the Moors and Christians fought by young boys. Special accessories and toys were made for the children—spears, swords, daggers and paper-headed horses on sticks. Small turbans, hats, robes and coats were worn by participants fighting the mock battle to the cry of "Moor or Christian?" Paper horses and a few toy swords may still appear in markets, but the battle is now seldom reenacted. There is, however, a masked folk dance based on this tradition called *Los Moros* performed in Michoacán, Papantla, Iguala and elsewhere on June 24.

Above and opposite page: Pink and yellow cut tissue paper banners, strung up as decorations on all festive occasions. 17″ × 13″ (43.2 × 33 cm.)

JULY

6

Indians in native costume gather to stage a unique hilltop ceremony to make offerings of hair and personal belongings on July 6th in Tlacotepec, Puebla.

8

In the village of Teotitlan del Valle in Oaxaca, practically every house is the workshop of one of the famous Oaxaca weavers, and a visit to the town is worthwhile just to see the weavers at work making woolen rugs, serapes and hangings. On July 8th every year the normally quiet square of the village is the scene of a fiesta where the colorful Feather Dances are performed.

16

This is a date celebrated all over Mexico on the occasion of the *Fiesta de la Virgen del Carmen.* It is a colorful festival held on July 16th, and it is especially well worth seeing at Oaxaca City, Ciudad del Carmen in Campeche and at Coyoacan.

Band made up of a father and four sons, ages 6 to 14 playing for a village fiesta at San Miguel de Allende.

Modern mold-made pottery *nacimiento* figures of the Three Kings bearing gifts. Painted in tempera colors and gold. Height 3¾″ (9.5 cm.)

Modern mold-made pottery *nacimiento* figures of the Holy Family. Height 2¾″ and 1⅞″ (7 and 4.8 cm.)

Castillo fireworks castle shooting off with vari-colored pinwheels whirling, to celebrate *el día de la Concepción* in front of the Church of the Conception in San Miguel de Allende, Guanajuato.

Clown—*payaso*—a fiesta fireworks piece turning slowly as yellow sparks shoot off. Construction made of split reed, papier maché, tissue and crêpe paper by Jaime Salvador of Oaxaca City. Height 46″ (1.17 m.)

Small modern ornamental mask (child's size) carved of copal wood, painted with enamel colors. The young wearer's eye holes are above the "real" eyes. 4½″ × 6″ (11.4 × 15.2 cm.)

Market woman and her baby standing with her market pots. Figure is tempera-painted pottery; pots are glazed and the tiny sets of platters in the foreground are painted and varnished. Woman is 4⅛″ tall (10.5 cm.), pots vary in height from ¼″ to 1⅜″ (0.6 to 4.1 cm.)

Huichol Indian votive object—
"Eye of God"—*ojo de dios.* A
rather neat, modern version of
this centuries-old beneficent
symbol made of wool yarn wound
on two crossed sticks. 7″ square
(17.8 cm.)

Adobe farm house near Etla,
Oaxaca.

Huichol Indian votive tablet called a *nearika*—wool yarn picture made on a wool panel coated with beeswax. The deer represents the sun, the most important Huichol diety. 5½″ × 7⅞″ (14 × 20 cm.)

Huichol Indian *nearika*, a yarn picture votive tablet representing the sun—a primary force in the Huichol beliefs. 6″ × 7⅞″ (15.2 × 20 cm.)

Huichol Indian *Chaquira*—a votive bowl made of half of a dried gourd lined with tiny glass beads set in beeswax in a symbolic design. This is not only one of the most handsome, but also the most significant of the altar offerings made to the Huichol gods in their sacred caves. Diameter 5½″ (14 cm.)

Children riding a crocodile, watched over by flying birds. A fanciful pottery toy painted in tempera colors. According to tradition, the Mexicans came [riding on a crocodile] from a mythical place, an island in the middle of a lake called Aztlán, whence the name *Aztecs.* (Soustelle, p. 253.) This reptile appears often as a folk toy of the country. Length 5½″, height 6¼″ (14 × 15.9 cm.)

Coyote carved of copal wood and painted with aniline colors; made by Manuel Jiménez, Arrasola, Oaxaca. The unique animation of Jiménez' animals can always be recognized. Length 13¾", height 7" (34.9 × 17.8 cm.)

Balloons—Mexico City.

Mask—large mold-made papier maché horned mask painted with tempera colors. This is a typical carnival mask—not worn over the face, but carried high on a stick by the cloth-covered reveler. Made in Celaya, Guanajuato. Height 11″, width 10″ (27.9 × 25.4 cm.)

Day of the Dead foods

Probably more varieties of traditional festive foods and confections are still made for the Day of the Dead on November second than for any other occasion, both for eating and to be used for grave offerings. Foods are made or purchased by people whether or not they participate in a ceremony at an altar or in a cemetary on this important date. Decorative loaves of bread called *panes de muertos* (bread of the dead) are small masterpieces of the baker's art baked only for this occasion in the shape of animals and men and women. The fancy loaves, some bun-sized and some larger are used for grave offerings, while much larger loaves with a sugar topping are made for general consumption. All these are produced only during the first week in November.

The *panes de muertos* made for grave or altar offerings differ from the ordinary white bread baked daily in every city and village of Mexico. The November second bread is made with whole-grained wheat flour, so it is dark in color, and the recipe includes eggs and a flavoring of anise, so it has a fine texture and a delicious, aromatic flavor. Decorations on the small, oval loaves are made with a plain white dough, and often the loaves have a white skull at one end and white feet at the other. The top and sides of the glazed "skeleton" loaf have ornamental scrolls and borders made of the same white dough.

A special sweet made for All Souls Day is called *alfeñique*—used principally for making decorative figures, but also to be eaten as a sugar paste when it is fresh and soft by candy-loving Mexicans of all ages. A sort of dough is made of potato starch, egg whites, sugar and lime juice; this is kneaded, then rolled out thin. It is then pressed into the two halves of various shapes of molds made of clay, plaster, wood or tin. When the sugar paste is almost dry, the two matching halves are taken out of the molds and fitted together and joined by more of the wet sugar dough. The process is almost identical to the molding of non-edible papier mâché and potter's clay. The dried, decorative finished pieces—skulls, skeletons, tombstones, fruit, flowers, figures and animals are tinted with vegetable colors and decorated with soft colored "frosting", sugar and tinsel. Details of finely-modeled paste, foil and ribbons are added to produce dozens and dozens of charming and unique little sculptures that are much too pretty to eat. Many are used to ornament the *ofrendas,* or Day of the Dead altars in homes and in cemeteries, and some quite large fruit and flower arrangements of *alfeñique* make imposing offerings in churches.

Loaves of bread for the Day of the Dead, made with dark flour and flavored with anise; decorated with white dough, and with a skeleton head and feet at the ends of the oval loaf. Made in Oaxaca City. 6¼″ × 8″ (15.9 × 20.3 cm.)

A home *ofrenda,* or offering altar in memory of the dead, with candlesticks, incense burner and three dishes of food; the reed arch is covered with *zempasúchitl,* the yellow-orange flower of the dead; the altar top is made of reeds.

Fruit made of *alfeñique* sugar paste, tinted in pastel colors and some coated with sugar. Arranged on a tin plate with small leaves to serve as an *ofrenda* or altar offering for the Day of the Dead—probably in memory of a child. Banana is 2¼″ long, apple is ⅞″ in diameter (5.7 and 2.2 cm.)

Man and woman, made of *alfeñique* sugar-paste, colored red, black, green with vegetable colors. Made for decorations for the Day of the Dead. Height 2¾″ (7 cm.)

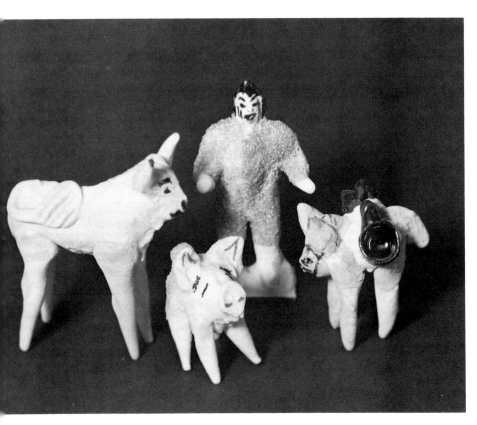

Group of small *alfeñique* sugar paste figures made for the Day of the Dead. The burro carries two small pots, and the man wears a suit of lavender sugar. Heights: man 2⅝″, pig 1⅜″ (6.7 and 3.5 cm.)

Angel—a figure made of bread, colored white, pink and green for an altar on the Day of the Dead. These elaborate bread figures are now seldom seem; this example is in the Regional Museum at Oaxaca.

The sugar-paste pieces, like the *panes de muertos*—bread of the dead—are made only during the first week of November, and principally by a few skilled women artisans in San Miguel de Allende, Guanajuato and in Toluca, Mexico. Fine examples of *alfeñique* can be seen in some museums—notably *el Alhondiga* in Guanajuato City—as they apparently harden and become more or less permanent sculptures.

Customs of the Day of the Dead

On the night of November first there are traditional ways to guide the souls of children to their homes or to an outdoor *ofrenda*. Parents sometimes shoot off firecrackers in front of the house to attract the attention of a child who may have lost his way. In country villages, a trail of yellow petals of the *zempasúchitl* flower is scattered from the child's grave to his home, or to the place near the cemetery where the family offering has been prepared, to guide the child's soul to the place where his people wait.

The orange-yellow flower called by its Náhuatl name, *zempasúchitl* (or *cempoalxochitl*) that grows wild in many areas of Mexico is the traditional flower of the dead. All graves, even those in the simplest country cemeteries are blanketed with these bright yellow marigold-like blossoms on November first and second. A double arch made of split bamboo or cane and laden with the yellow-orange flowers is often set over a grave and looks like a small, golden chapel-tower. A night vigil is kept at the cemetery with candles burning on the decorated graves, and in both Catholic and Indian communities it is an impressive sight.

Hundreds of people visit cemeteries all day long during this two-day festival. Priests are there to bless graves, and visitors sit at graveside, praying. Outside the cemetery wall or fence there is a subdued but happy atmosphere with street stalls selling flowers, food and drinks, *alfeñique* and other confections. The people socialize and visit together, after their communing with the dead has been done quietly at the grave.

Skull, mold-made of *alfeñique* sugar paste, painted with vegetable colors, red, black, blue. 3¼″ × 4¾″ (8.3 × 12.1 cm.)

Offering to the Dead on primitive graves in the cemetery at Chilac, Puebla.

131

Skeleton doll made of painted papier-maché—mold-pressed in two pieces joined with a metal wire spring neck; black, white and red. 14½" tall (36.8 cm.)

The list of toys and other objects made for the Day of the Dead is extensive. Dolls, masks and miniatures with myriad representations of skulls and skeletons are made of all kinds of materials by craftsmen throughout Mexico for living children to enjoy. These are as acceptable to *muchachas* and *muchachos* as a doll with a wardrobe or a wind-up truck is to a North American girl and boy. Playthings include skeleton miniatures of many kinds, jumping jacks and puppets made of tin, clay or wood, papier mâché masks, skeleton dolls of all kinds and sizes, miniature *ofrendas* stacked with food, small coffins bearing a skeleton that jumps out when a string is pulled and miniature funeral processions with chick-pea-headed paper figures carrying a coffin.

So, the child's first acquaintance with death—even if he does not understand it at an early age—is a natural and cheerful one. The Spanish word for skull is *calavera,* but an indication of how lightly the word is taken in Mexico is that the same word in slang means "a dead guy," a "daredevil," a "scapegoat," or a kind of late nineteenth century printed broadside. Octavio Paz says, "The word death is not pronounced in New York, Paris, or in London, because it burns the lips. The Mexican, in contrast, is familiar with death, jokes about it, caresses it, sleeps with it, celebrates it; it is one of his favorite toys and his most steadfast love. True, there is perhaps as much fear in his attitude as that of theirs, but at least death is not hidden away: he looks at it face to face, with impatience, disdain or irony."*

There is a difference between the way the Day of the Dead is marked by sophisticated city people and the observance of the occasion by country and village dwellers, especially in Indian communities. Diego Rivera's two *día de los Muertos* fresco paintings in the Ministry of Education building in Mexico City portray the difference graphically. In his "city" painting people are chatting, eating and drinking with skull-faced figures hooded and dressed in black while three large puppet-like death figures play guitars in the background. It is a mocking and irreverent scene with a staged, theatrical quality. In Rivera's "country" Day of the Dead painting, Indians are kneeling devoutly before a candle-lit altar and at decorated graves, making an impressive scene much like the one still enacted each year on Janitzio Island.

*Paz, *The Labyrinth of Solitude,* p. 57.

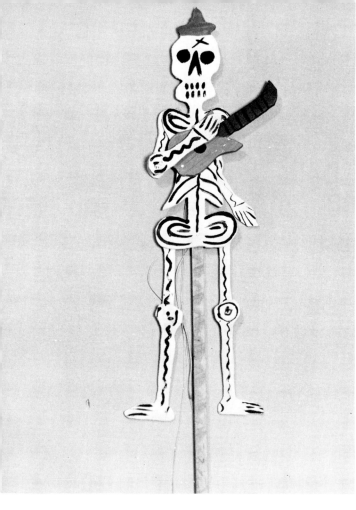

Skeleton jumping jack made of painted wood, wearing a red hat and playing a red and green guitar. Height 12″ (30.5 cm.)

Extended skeleton jumping jack.

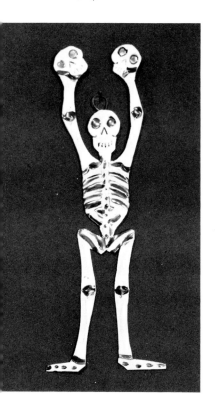

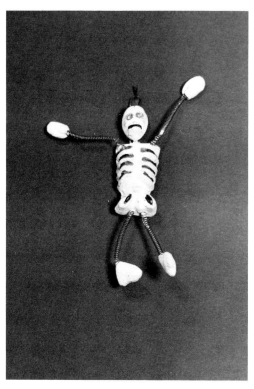

Tin skeleton holding skulls; height 6″ (15.2 cm.) *Center:* Painted clay and spring wire skeleton; height 3″ (7.6 cm.)

Right: Traffic policeman skeleton with whistle in his mouth, standing on typical Mexican traffic "box"; mold-made pottery painted with tempera colors, brown uniform, black, white and yellow. Height 3¾″ (9.5 cm.)

Four metal cuts by José Guadalupe Posada from a series of
calaveras (broadsides) called "The Big Cemetery of Lovers"
published for the Day of the Dead around the year 1900.

From about 1868 to 1910, verses and songs called *calaveras* were printed on handbills and sold for a few centavos in the streets of Mexico City, especially in November. Many of these were illustrated with powerful woodcuts by José Guadalupe Posada (who died in 1913) and all had satirical subjects mocking death as well as ridiculing unpopular public figures. Posada also illustrated current events in broadsides, and made covers for books and music. The boldness of Posada's work greatly influenced two younger Mexican artists, Diego Rivera and José Orozco, whose now-famous paintings use similar satirical themes.

In past years a traditional play was performed in small theaters in Mexico at the time of the Day of the Dead. It was called *Don Juan Tenorio,* or Don Juan the Lady Killer, written by José Zorilla, and long a favorite in Spain. It is still performed in some cities in November.

Many Mexican Catholics, some of whom are of partly Indian descent, still retain the deep-rooted beliefs that involve ceremonies on *el día de los Muertos* that are as much pagan as they are Christian. The combination of doctrines is said to have brought about a point of view toward death that is distinctive, as Paz said. Many philosophers have written about the Mexicans' uniquely fatalistic acceptance of death. This may have been a prevalent attitude a number of years ago, and of course still exists to some degree, but is probably now much less common. As long as thirty-five years ago, the American sociologist, Oscar Lewis, pointed out in the recorded words of the people in this book, *A Death in the Sanchez Family* that a philosophical acceptance of death did not exist among the impoverished people living on the fringes of Mexico City.

The elements of fear and dread were traditionally said not to be a part of the Mexican's anticipation of the end of life, for he knew that the soul remains alive forever. If a cordial feeling toward his departed relatives and friends provides the Mexican with a kind of reassurance about his own death, this cannot easily be shared by people who take a different view of dying. But it is certainly possible to admire and even to envy a philosophy that to some degree makes death an acceptable end of life, no matter how grievous the loss may be when it occurs.

Dog Skeleton carved of unpainted copal wood by *Gordo,* a country carver whose work is very primitive. San Martin Tilcajete; Height 4½" (11.4 cm.)

Mask, papier maché mold-made skull; painted black, white, red and metallic gold. 6¾" × 8¼" (17.1 × 21 cm.)

Skeleton one-string puppet. Head, chest, hands and feet made of clay, held together by and glued to the purple cloth costume. Height 6″ (15.2 cm.)

Indian Day of The Dead Ceremonies

The Zapotecs of Oaxaca

These Indians, living in south central Mexico still practice age-old ceremonies, but they have some of their own ideas about the dead. They believe that all the souls of their dead "live" in ancient tombs at Mitla, a nearby important archeological site, and that the spirits leave the tombs to visit their families on November second and share the food that has been prepared for them.

The Zapotecs ascribe a realistic presence to the returning souls, and show some fear of them. The Indians know that it is imperative to light many candles because they believe the spirits will weep continuously until each one's way is lighted. Many natives make an effort to stay safely in their homes on November first and second because they do not like the idea of meeting a wandering spirit at night. Some try not to go to sleep at all during the two nights of the festival because they fear that their sleep might be mistaken for death, in which case the spirits would take them to the tomb. These Oaxacan Indians also want to make sure that all souls have returned to their tombs after visiting, and rituals are carried out to clear away any spirits that are lost or who might have chosen to stay with the living to haunt them. Priests and musicians go about the village on November third, chanting and intoning prayers to get rid of remaining spirits.

The Mayas of Yucatán

The Mayas believe that only the good souls are allowed to come back to visit their families, and that they may come at any time during the first seven days of November, starting with the *angelitos* on the first. Morning and midday meals are offered to the children's souls at the church, and at night a candle is lighted on each child's grave so that he can find his way back to it. A similar ceremony is performed for other visiting souls, and a festive farewell ritual and feast are held at the end of the week. No candles are lighted for the older spirits, since it is supposed they can find their own way back to their graves in the dark.

Archeological ruins at Mitla, near Oaxaca City—the site where the Zapotec Indians believe their dead are entombed.

The Tarascans of Janitzio Island

This small island in Lake Pátzcuaro in the state of Michoacán is the setting for one of the most impressive Day of the Dead ceremonies in Mexico. The cemetery and church of this small fishing village are high on the summit of a stony hill on which the houses are built. This situation provides a dramatic setting for the candle-lighting ceremony on the night of November second.

The Tarascan Indians believe that the souls of the dead come down from the cemetary to visit their families in the evening. Then, at midnight, the village women and children, wearing festive native dress, walk up the steeply winding paths to the graves, accompanied by the spirits. The children carry flowers and the women carry flower arches, baskets of food and a candle for each soul. The offerings and candles are placed on the graves, the hundreds of candles are lighted and an all-night vigil begins. The men and boys of town quietly gather around the edges of the cemetery and sing songs of praise to the dead. At dawn, the spirits return to their graves, the food is eaten, then all the people enter the cemetery church where the Catholic priest says a mass for the dead. The beautiful ceremony is a combination of Tarascan and Christian rituals.

Summary

No grand memorial constructed to honor the memory of a human can quite evoke the feeling of remembrance equal to that manifested on the Day of the Dead in the traditional Indian ceremonies of Mexico, when candles are lighted and all departed souls are warmly received by their families.

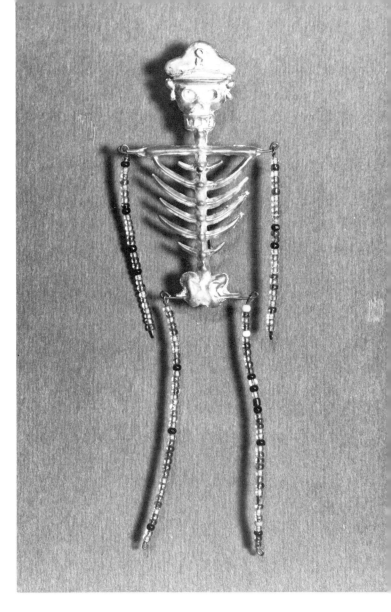

Skeleton pin made of lead with beaded wire arms and legs; to be worn as a decoration on the Day of the Dead. The figure wears a policeman's hat and his ribs are rather upside down. Height 4″ (10.2 cm.)

20

Mexico celebrates its Independence Day on the anniversary of the revolution of 1910, the 20th of November.

DECEMBER

8

Even before the solemnity and festivity of Christmas begin in Mexico, there are many local and some national festivals. December eighth is the Feast of the Immaculate Conception, an occasion that is

Janitzio Island, site of the Tarascan Indian ceremonies on the Day of the Dead. The giant statue of Morelos is next to the cemetery on the top of the island hill.

the name-day of all girls and women called *Concepción*, and of every Catholic church of that name. There are church services, socializing, music, sometimes native dancing, and finally fireworks—rockets, balloons and the *castillo*. The fireworks castle is sometimes set up in the church plaza, and sometimes in the street. The whole village turns out to watch the colorful climax to a happy day.

In some towns, and especially in Pátzcuaro, December eighth is celebrated in churches as the *Fiesta de la Virgen de Salud,* our Mother of Health. After religious services there used to be an all-day fiesta distinguished by the appearance of unique characters called *monigotes,* grotesque figures who were youths dressed in long white robes, wearing large masks and walking about on tall stilts, to amuse the children. And, of course, at night there are fireworks.

The original Basilica of Guadalupe at Tepeyac, on the outskirts of Mexico City. The structure has sunk about six feet into the sandy sub-soil of the city.

Guadalupe—the new shrine, the old basilica and old shrine. This site at Tepeyac was originally the site of the sanctuary of *Tonantzin,* the revered mother of the Aztecs. The Spaniards chose to build the first shrine on this site in the year 1787. The new shrine (the circular structure) is in use, but was not quite completed in 1977.

12

December 12th has been celebrated for over four hundred years in all the Catholic churches of Mexico as the Day of the Virgin of Guadelupe—the country's patroness saint. In the year 1531 the Virgin Mary is said to have appeared in a vision before a humble Indian boy named Juan Diego and commanded him to see that a church be built where Indians could worship freely. The church and shrine of the Virgin of Guadelupe were eventually built in Tepeyac, a village on the edge of Mexico City. The annual pilgrimage of thousands of worshipers to her principal shrine has become one of the religious spectacles of Mexico. In recent years the original shrine has been sinking into the sandy soil and falling into disrepair, and it cannot even begin to accommodate the pilgrims, so a new, much larger modern shrine has been built nearby, and was used for the first time in 1976 as the center of worship.

16

The state of Oaxaca celebrates a special fiesta during the first three days of the official Christmas season—December 16th to 18th, in honor of its patroness, *la Virgen de la Soledad*. The principal site of the processions is at the Soledad Church in Oaxaca City.

Posadas and Piñatas

On December 16th the nation-wide Mexican celebration of Christmas really begins with the nine days of Christmas. Plazas and public buildings begin to be decorated with lanterns, colored paper banners and festoons of moss. In homes, the family sets up its *nacimiento,* or crêche, with small figures portraying the scene with the Holy Family in Bethlehem. These activities are never begun before the 16th of the month. That evening, in most of the villages and towns of Mexico the first of the nine *posadas* is held, and most of these are followed by a *piñata* party. These traditional religious processions and gay fiestas are sometimes arranged for all to enjoy, but there are many *barrio,* or neighborhood *posadas* arranged by small groups of friends which culminate in private homes with refreshments and a *piñata*-breaking party for the children.

The *posadas* (literally: inns) have their origin in the Bible and are the reenactment of the journey taken by the Holy Family from Nazareth to Bethlehem, and of their search for shelter. The Spanish missionaries in Mexico in the 16th century found that a most important Aztec feast had been celebrated during the nine days before the Christmas nativity date, and the pageant of the Biblical journey is said to have been taught to the converts to "replace" the pagan ceremonies of the same period.

As enacted in the very early days of the Mexican Republic, *posadas* have been described in charming

Tissue paper banners flying over the main street of Puerto Vallarta, Jalisco at Christmas time, 1974.

Engraving portraying a nineteenth century *posada*.

139

Father and son musicians at a fiesta.

detail in a book called *Life in Mexico* written in 1840. The author was the Scottish wife of Spain's first Minister to Mexico, Don Angel Calderón de Barca. Fanny Calderón's 19th century *posada* was described as follows:

24

"This is the last night of what are called the *Posadas,* a curious mixture of religion and amusement, but extremely pretty. The meaning is this: when the Virgin and Joseph, having come out of Galilee, found Bethlehem so full of people that they wandered about for nine days, without finding admittance in any house or tavern and on the ninth day, took shelter in a manger, where the Saviour was born. For eight days this wandering of the Holy Family to the different *posadas* is represented, and seems more intended for an amusement to the children than anything serious. We went to the Marquesa's at eight o'clock, and about nine the ceremony commenced. A lighted taper is put into the hand of each lady, and a procession was formed, two by two, which marched through the house, the corridors and walls of which were all decorated with evergreens and lamps, the whole party singing the Litanies. K. walked with the dowager Marquesa; and a group of little children dressed as angels joined the procession. They wore little robes of silver or gold lamé, plumes of white feathers, and a profusion of fine diamonds and pearls in *bandeaux,* brooches and necklaces, white gauze wings, and white satin shoes embroidered in gold.

"At last the procession drew up before a door and a shower of fireworks was sent flying over our heads. I suppose to represent the descent of the angels; for a group of ladies appeared dressed to represent the shepherds who watched their flocks by night upon the plains of Bethlehem. Then voices supposed to be those of Mary and Joseph struck up a hymn, in which they begged for admittance, saying that the night was cold and dark, that the wind blew hard, and that they prayed for a night's shelter. A chorus of voices from within refused admittance. Again, those without entreated shelter, and at length declared that she at the door, who thus wandered in the night, and had not where to lay her head, was the Queen of Heaven! At this name the doors were thrown wide open, and the Holy Family entered singing. The scene within was very pretty: a *nacimiento.* Platforms going all around the room were covered with moss on which were disposed groups of wax figures generally representing passages from different parts of the New Testament, though sometimes they began with Adam and Eve in Paradise. There was the Annunciation—the Salutation of Mary to Elizabeth—the Wise Men of the East—the Shepherds—the Flight into Egypt. There were green trees and fruit trees, and little fountains that cast up fairy columns of water, and flocks of sheep, and a little cradle in

Village Feather Dancers at a fiesta at San Miguel de Allende.

"Matachines"

140

which to lay the infant Christ. One of the angels held a waxen baby in her arms. The whole was lighted very brilliantly, and ornamented with flowers and garlands. A padre took the baby from the Angel and placed it in the cradle, and the *posada* was completed.

"We then returned to the drawing room—angels, shepherds and all, and danced till suppertime. The supper was a show for sweetmeats and cakes."*

The *posadas* are said to have begun in Mexico as early as 1587, although the *piñata* game was not reported to be a part of this Christmas Eve ceremony in an elegant nineteenth century home. It was possibly the simple people of the villages who enjoyed the game most at first, and who still do.

In reenacting the *posada* today, a procession of village people, usually dressed in simple robes, goes through the streets at night, each person carrying a lighted candle. They are led by a young girl on a burro representing the Virgin, and she is escorted by a man representing Joseph. Sometimes painted plaster figures are carried to represent these two from the Bible, along with figures of guardian angels. The group sings a long litany telling of the search of Joseph and Mary for lodging, and the chanted responses of the innkeepers. After being denied shelter several times, the group is finally admitted (by prearrangement) to a welcoming house and there is rejoicing as the procession ends.

The hospitable reception nowadays nearly always includes the game of breaking the *piñata*—another traditional custom with a long but separate history. Its origins are uncertain, but the idea may have been brought first to Italy from the Orient by Marco Polo. The Spanish copied the diversion from the Italians who played their game with a clay pot called a *pignatta*, hence the name. It was then an entertainment for nobles and ladies of the sixteenth or seventeenth century who hoped to gather up some of the jewels and baubles with which their host had filled the breakable pot. The game is now played in Mexico in exactly the same way as in Italy, and later in Spain, where it became a Lenten custom. For the Italian dukes and duchesses, the rewards were of some value, compared to the sweets and toys now garnered by Mexican children. In Mexico, a plain, round clay cooking pot called an *olla* is decorated and finally almost entirely concealed by ruffles and streamer coverings shaped into animals, stars, etc. It is filled with nuts, sugar cane, fruits and

*Calderon de la Barca.

Piñatas hanging outside shop at Taxco; deer and giraffe.

Clay cooking pots—*ollas*—red bisque on the outside and green-glazed inside. These are the Indians' common pots for cooking beans—they are poured in a mold, and turned out by the hundreds as a cheap kitchen necessity. *Ollas* like these are used as the center of piñatas. Diameter 13" (33 cm.)

Piñata, white cock made of white tissue paper and colored foil details. The feet are made of tightly-rolled newspaper covered with foil. Made by the Vasquez family of San Miguel. Height 29″, width 24″ (73.7 × 61 cm.)

Piñata, snow-man—the Vasquez interpretation of the Christmas symbol from far north of Mexico, made with two *ollas* and a paper head. Decorations are carefully interpreted in colored foil. Height 29″ (73.7 cm.)

small toys and is hung overhead from a rope. One participant in the game is blindfolded and given a long stick with which he or she tries to hit the pot. Several people (usually children) take turns at being blindfolded and swinging the stick, and finally when someone hits the pot hard enough to break it, the other players scramble on the ground for the scattered prizes. It is a kind of noisy and happy version of a grab-bag, and the game goes on for quite a few minutes, since a controlling cord is used to swing the pot out of reach of the batters. There are several sing-song chants which the children say as the game goes on with each new target. One of them says:

No quiero oro,	I don't want gold
No quiero plata,	I don't want silver
Lo que yo quiero	What I want is
Es romper la piñata.	To break the piñata.

Those who seek Christian symbolism that might connect the piñata with the Christmas season say that the decorated pot represents the spirit of evil, the goodies are symbolic of temptation and the blindfolded player is the child's blind faith that destroys evil. Light-hearted youngsters taking a swing at the piñata are surely not aware of this ponderous interpretation!

Piñatas

This is a Christmas fiesta toy that is still alive and well in Mexico. The pretty hanging ornaments may be found in the markets of many towns beginning about the middle of December. The best ones are made in the traditional way, using a round *olla*, or clay cooking pot, as the core around which a split reed or bamboo and cardboard framework is constructed in the shape of many things: six or eight-pointed stars, parrots, peacocks, burros, elephants, fish and other creatures. Over the pot and its surrounding framework the shape is formed in papier mâché, usually made of salvaged cement bags of heavy brown paper, torn into scraps and soaked in flour and water paste. This "skin" is then covered with rows and rows of frilly tissue paper ruffles and decorated with foil, colored papers and streamers.

Piñata-making is usually a family enterprise involving four or five adult members of a family and cluttering up most of the space in a small house. One grandmother in San Miguel de Allende who does much of the tedious cutting of the yards and yards

142

of paper ruffles that are pasted on the surface and are so important to the appearance of a good *piñata* demonstrated how she could cut the tissue paper very neatly, with her eyes closed! Paste, string and wire are used to fasten the whole construction together, and it takes about two hours for four experienced craftspeople working at separate parts of the process to complete the average-sized *piñata*. In San Miguel five members of the Vasquez family are expert *piñata* makers and produced all the pieces shown in the photographs except the two shown hanging outside a shop in Taxco. Many people now use *piñatas* as bright Christmas ornaments to hang anywhere in the house, and they would not think of allowing them to be smashed at a party. (See color plates)

Detail of the head of the peacock *piñata* (shown also in a color plate) with the extremely fine-cut ruffles used for this impressive bird.

Piñata, eight-pointed star with purple foil points and pink tissue paper ruffles and streamers. Made by the Vasquez family of San Miguel de Allende. Width 31″ (78.7 cm.)

24

Posadas and *piñata*-breaking festivities are repeated every night until *Noche Buena,* Christmas Eve, when the Christ Child figure is added for the first time to both the *posada* and the *nacimiento* manger; never before. In some towns the final *posada* ends at the door of the church where the participants enter and hear the midnight mass said by the priest. In the hilltown village of Taxco, the Christmas Eve *posada,* with many participants carrying lighted candles and singing as they wind their way down from the hills by narrow streets toward the church plaza, ends in the magnificent Santa Prisca church which—on this one occasion—is entirely illuminated by the light of hundreds of candles.

La Pastorela

The Christmas pastoral playlet became popular in colonial days; it was brought to Mexico by the Spanish, but its origin goes back to the religious theater of the Middle Ages. The folk plays were written in verse by anonymous writers and they always have a cast of symbolic characters like innocent shepherds and children, devils, archangels, the Three Kings and the Holy Family in Bethlehem. Good always triumphs over evil as village people, often garbed in native or local dress, play their parts. Pastorals may be seen during Christmas week— usually sponsored by a church, academy or school. These descendants of early morality plays are sometimes quite charmingly staged in a patio or cloister, and are performed free to everyone. Even children can enjoy the simple stories and broad humor of

143

Carmen Vasquez, *piñata*-maker.   Juana Vasquez, *piñata*-maker.

Ricardo Vasquez, master *piñata*-maker of San Miguel de Allende.

The Vasquez children playing in the court of the *piñata* maker's house. The children are laughing at the boy with his back to us because he is not wearing any *pantalones* for a visitor with a camera.

these traditional performances. The plays sometimes conclude with the singing of Christmas carols in which the audience joins the players.

Sweets and Decorations

There is a traditional sweet for the Christmas season in Mexico. *Buñuelos* are large, flaky pastries with cinnamon and brown sugar syrup which are sold in flat pottery dishes by street vendors, especially on Christmas Eve. It is customary for the dishes from which the confection has been eaten to be thrown down and broken—for good luck.

The villages in Mexico are gaily decorated for Christmas—mainly the church plazas and parks. The dependably dry and mild weather permits the use of fragile colored tissue paper chains, painted lanterns, moss, palm leaves, real or paper flowers and ribbons. Except in Mexico City, strings of tiny lights, neon, tinsel and plastic decorations, Christmas trees and Santa Claus figures are not often seen in Mexico. The all-important *nacimiento* is set up in most homes, in store windows, in hotel lobbies and in the central plaza of the town. The latter is sometimes a very extensive and charming, if rather hodge-podge collection of wood and pottery figures and animals, the Holy Family in a shelter, the Three Kings, palm trees, waterfalls, a star overhead and a great deal of Spanish moss. Some of the figures may be one inch tall and some a foot or more in height. No matter; the scene is rendered as if it were a part of the environment of the country life of Mexico and its people. The *nacimiento* is painstakingly put together and it is much admired.

Mexico City has for years been a spectacular sight at Christmas time; there are wonderful life-sized papier mâché fairy tale figures, and sometimes Mary, Joseph and the Wise Men and their animals set up in Alameda Park—the central family park of the city. Unfortunately, sometimes the displays are American-cartoon inspired, are accompanied by recorded music, and have no Mexican quality at all. In the *zócalo*—the large square surrounded by government buildings and the cathedral—enormous constructions with lights blaze away, and these are of different design every year. All the main streets downtown are decorated and lighted, and many *barrios* install their own street decorations. All of these have a special Mexican style and do not look much like the plastic pine, bells and tinsel decorations in a North American city. There is an unselfconsciousness to Mexican decorations, even on this all-important occasion. The city in all its Christmas glory is well worth seeing.

CHRISTMAS AND NEW YEAR

24-25

Christmas Eve is celebrated in fiesta fashion in many places—especially if there is no *posada;* if there are fireworks they always end before the midnight mass. Christmas Day, without the excitement of exchanging gifts, is a rather quiet holiday compared to the events of the preceding weeks in Mexico. There are family dinners at home and always attendance at church to pay homage to the Christ Child. Country people come to town dressed in their best finery and stroll around in the parks in the afternoon and evening.

28

December 28th is celebrated as the Feast of the Holy Innocents, which supposedly originated in the mocking of Herod. It has become a day for practical jokes, tricks and pranks among children who consider this date to be their holiday. In some markets there are special small tin trays loaded with a collection of miniature objects—one tray for girls and another for boys.

Fireworks

Fireworks may be called the favorite toy of Mexico, and there is a calendar full of occasions on which fireworks are used during the year.

In many locations, Christmas is the season when displays of this brilliant, explosive art are the most elaborate and impressive of all. The *pirotécnicos* and *coheteros* who make fireworks are important artisans with highly special skills, not to mention a bit of daring. Nowadays they must all be licensed to handle explosives, but there is as yet no prohibition of their products. There is an old story about the *pirotécnico* who used his *machete* to cut up lengths of explosives—like chopping carrots with a knife; this casual approach to the pursuit of his work may or may not be a thing of the past.

Not every town boasts a fireworks maker, but there is always one in a nearby community, and he is a very busy person when preparations for a fiesta must begin. Only small firecrackers, sparklers, and those crackling little explosives that skitter about underfoot (*buscapies,* or "foot-searchers") can be bought in the markets. Rockets, balloons and bombs are made to order for a town, a park, a church, or for whomever sponsors the display.

145

Modern-day children at a piñata party.

Angel, papier maché covered with foil, partly painted; one of a number of life-size figures set up as a *nacimiento*, or Christmas crèche, using the natural setting of Alameda Park in Mexico City in 1967. Height about 5' (1.52 m.)

An eighteenth century engraving showing two *castillos* set up in the zócalo of Mexico City to celebrate the beatification of San Felipe de Jesus, February 5, 1629.

Men starting construction of a free-standing *castillo*, Taxco, Guerrero, 1972.

The two largest and most complicated fireworks pieces are the *castillo*, or castle, and the Judas figures of earlier times; the latter are described in chapter V under the month of March. The *castillo* is literally a castle-tower of fireworks about thirty or more feet high (9.14 m.) that may take three men as long as eight days to build, another full day to fit with fireworks, another day to set up—and about twenty minutes to go off. It is a masterpiece of delicate engineering with a light wood or reed framework to which an incredibly complicated assortment of carefully wrapped and connected fireworks are attached. These flame and scatter in a rainbow of colors as they shoot, spin, explode, sizzle, screech, pop, float, flare and boom when they go off.

The castillo

Pictured here are *castillos* before and during the shoot-off; the construction of the *castillo* is interesting, and the framework is often in itself a work of art. The light, open construction may be made of narrow, painted strips of wood, or more often, of split reed or bamboo in its natural color. The pieces are fastened together with wrappings of very fine wire. The open, cage-like sections of the tower, which will be stacked one on top of another, or fastened around a pole at intervals, are between 20 to 30 inches wide and about 18 to 25 inches high (51 cm. to 1 m. wide and about 46 to 64 cm. high.) In a free-standing tower (described later) the lower sections are wider than those at the top. Each section is carefully put together, then strung with the explosives in the *pirotécnico's* patio workshop. The intricately-designed framework for the sections may be used over and over again with new explosives, as they do not burn up during firing. Pin-wheels or Catherine wheels are also made and strung separately, then attached to the tower. The topmost section usually differs in shape from the other cubes and it will have a powerful aerial bomb, rocket or hot air balloon that will go off in a spectacular climax after the shoot-off has slowly worked its way up the castle.

On the day of the fiesta, all the pieces of the *castillo* are transported by truck to the site of the celebration. The three or more men who have spent better than a week's time attaching the explosives to the already-built sections of the tower not only now have to connect all the sections and parts of the tower to each other, but also they must join all the explosives on them into one continuous chain, with no breaks of any sort between connections. The castles may be put together in one of two ways—and both take all day to accomplish. The usual way is to lay a sturdy pole about two and one half feet longer than the *castillo's* height in a horizontal position on supports, and "string" the sections onto the pole, fastening them to it and to each other as they are added. About sun-down the job is done, and the finished tower is lifted and carried on the shoulders of the workmen to the hole where it will be set up and secured. The hole for the pole is usually made by simply removing a paving stone from the street or plaza, and digging a hole in the earth deep enough to hold the tower in place. With much shouting and straining and amateur help, the pole is raised to its vertical position, dropped into place, clamped into a metal tripod at the base and secured with guy wires.

Another more difficult method is used to construct *castillos* that are so tall that they must be raised without a center pole—these are lighter in weight. In this case, the fireworks-strung sections are assembled in the final location, starting with the top piece, lifting it and setting the next cage under it, wiring and connecting these two together, setting a third cage under the second, and so on until the whole tower of fifteen or twenty connected sections is erected. Many steadying guy wires secured in all directions are necessary to hold this castle in place, because the whirling and shooting explosions of the *castillo* set up quite a strong shuddering motion.

When all is ready for the performance, a prelude of smaller fireworks are shot off by the same *cohetero* and his assistants, beginning at about 10 P.M. First there are a few rockets (held by hand and lighted with a cigarette) sent up to burst in a shower of stars. The people respond with squeals and sighs. Then a paper balloon with a lighted candle inside is inflated and sent up. Then more rockets, then suddenly a frantic, sputtering "fire" that travels on a wire at breakneck speed across the plaza and back again, whooshing over the heads of the people in the crowd and shooting off green sparks as it goes. Then more and more rockets, balloons and traveling *fuegos*.

Finally comes the feature act; the *castillo* fuse is lighted and a small sputter of sparks begins at the bottom of the structure, and the colorful, noisy exhibition begins. As each section slowly ignites and blows, whirls, smokes or sizzles, the crowd cheers. Red flames, yellow sparks, pinwheels, green flares, blue stars and dozens of other variations go off, one after another, slowly creeping up the four sides, rounding corners one at a time, climbing ever higher until the aerial bomb goes off at the top

147

Center section of *castillo* under construction at Taxco.

Finished *castillo* showing guy wires; strung with fireworks and ready for the Christmas Eve show, 1972.

Castillo.

making a huge shower of stars more than a hundred feet overhead. Then the big colorful balloon inflates, detaches itself and floats off into the night sky. The twenty-minute show is over. (See color plate)

The *cohetero* stands almost under the tower watching the progress of each succeeding act that he has planned so carefully. He smiles broadly as sparks bounce off him and all around him during the whole show. Most people watching do not even know who the dark, happy little man is—the artist of this spectacular creation.

Sometimes on very special occasions two *castillos* are set up for the same celebration. They are usually built by two different *pirotécnicos* in an air of friendly competition, and they are set off one after the other. Always, the two castles give a very different effect when they are fired, so that it is possible to see graphically the skills in timing, color and design required for this art. Some visitors who travel in Mexico without a fiesta calendar have visited the country several times, and have never seen this most Mexican of all the explosive creations.

The Torito

The little bull of Mexico is not associated with a specific festival, but it may be a part of any one of them. It is seen less and less often now, since the number of *coheteros* who can make it appears to be decreasing. This fireworks toy has its origin in the Spanish bullfight, but it was probably a Mexican idea to fit a small cane and paper bull with fireworks solely for the entertainment of celebrants at a fiesta. The *torito* is so familiar and so much-liked in Mexico that it is customarily used as the identifying shop-sign on the front of the house of the fireworks maker.

To make the little bull's figure, a rather delicate split cane framework is constructed, tied together with cord and wire, and made so that it stands on four extended cane stick legs. The skeleton is then covered with papier mâché, and shaped like a bull's body, except that the bottom is left open. Then paper ears and horns are added and colored tissue paper and paint are applied overall, to indicate eyes, spots and a ribbon around the neck. When the figure is completed, a separate bamboo construction is made that will be fitted over and attached to the bull's back. It is topped with a sort of decorative arch that will make the whole figure about 44 inches (1.12 m.) high. This light superstructure is wound with

Author with master-*pirotécnico,* Francisco Ortega-Ramos.

148

explosives and fitted with three pinwheels, one on each side and one at the rear. Touches of fluttery tissue paper are added to the arch, the fuse is attached, the arch is tied in place on the bull's back, and the *torito* is ready to go.

Shooting off a *torito* is really a spree or a game played with great relish by the *cohetero,* and enjoyed with squeals and much running about by the people—especially the children. The fuse is lighted, the fireworks maker, who is now the performer, picks up the bull and puts it over his head, holds on to the two front legs and tilts the animal back just far enough so that he can see where he is going. The fireworks start sputtering and exploding, shooting out sparks and colored fire in slow progression in the same way as those of the *castillo.* The man now pretends to be a charging bull, and heads into the crowd with sparks flying. Everybody scatters, shouting and laughing; then he makes another lunge and keeps repeating his wild running about with pinwheels spinning and small rockets shooting off until the fireworks are finished. It is a very noisy and colorful bullfight while it lasts, and the excitement is heightened by the danger that someone may get burned, but nothing really serious seems to happen to anybody. For a few seconds the whole scene is bright red, then a green flare replaces the red. (See color plates)

As with the castle, the framework stays intact and may be used for another set of fireworks at another fiesta. The little bull itself is usually singed only slightly and can be patched up and re-used.

Turtles, dolls and clowns

A few other fireworks toys are traditional in Mexico—each working in a slightly different way than the castle and the bull. The *tortuga,* turtle, is an animal that has been portrayed in many forms since pre-conquest days. It is another favorite fireworks toy whose figure for fiestas is constructed in the same way as the little bull, but it is only about 20 inches (51 cm.) in length, and the finished turtle may be set on wheels, or made so that its head and tail will move. When the fuse is lighted, the wheeled turtle is propelled by a series of small rockets so that he travels along the plaza in a slow, fiery walk. Or his head will start slowly wagging back and forth, then his tail will wag. *Muñecas* and *payasos*—dolls and clowns from about 18 inches to 40 inches tall (45.7 cm. to 1.015 m.) are also constructed of papier mâché, crêpe and tissue paper, decorated with paint,

Torito—closeup of face.

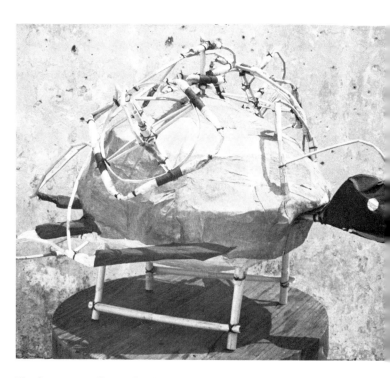

Turtle—*tortuga*—figure, fitted with fireworks; body: green tissue paper-covered papier maché, head: black. Made by Jaime Salvador of Oaxaca. Length 31″, width 21″, height 20″ (78.7 × 53.3 × 50.8 cm.)

149

strung with fireworks and are sometimes put on wheels so they will twirl. The little figures appear to come to sparkling life as they move or turn when the fireworks go off. Unlike the Judas figures of Holy Saturday, which were wired with loud and destructive explosives, these small figures are only meant to be animated and colorful, with a display of fireworks attached outside them, like the little bull. They are not destroyed by their performances. (See color plate)

These charming and diverting (if short-lived) toys are now rarely seen and the men who have the skill to make them are becoming fewer and fewer. The only places such toys are apt to be found are in the glass cases of popular arts museums. The museum, *El Alhondiga* in Guanajuato City has an extensive collection, the museum at Oaxaca has a few pieces; some fireworks toys are shown occasionally in special exhibitions at the two popular arts showroom-museums on Juarez Boulevard in Mexico City. The museum at No. 92 Juarez has some notable huge Judas figures (shown in our photographs.) The torito, clown and turtle pictured here were made to order especially for this book, and were shot off in a field in Etla, Oaxaca for the enjoyment of the authors and a few friends.

Fireworks turtle—*tortuga*—made by Jaime Salvador of Oaxaca. The little turtle is shooting off with head and tail wagging.

The fireworks clown made by Jaime Salvador, shooting off and turning around as he stands on a reed pole stuck into the ground. Red flares are going off.

Summary

Mexico's Catholics are devoutly religious, and so are Mexico's Indians—in their own way. All have great reverance for their religious occasions and celebrate them gravely; all have tolerance for the others.

But fiestas, with the excitement of their color, dancing, music, toys and decorations are for everybody, and are not only a truly Mexican expression, but they are, in fact, an essential part of the life of the ordinary persons. Octavio Paz tells us: "It is impossible to calculate how many fiestas we have and how much time and money are spent on them. I remember asking the mayor of a village near Mitla, 'What is the income of the village government?' 'About 3,000 pesos a year (then $240.00). We are very poor. But the Governor and the Federal Government always help to meet our expenses.' 'And how are the 3,000 pesos spent?' 'Mostly on fiestas, señor; we are a small village, but we have two patron saints.'*

Note: most of the calendar dates in this chapter are taken from Norman's *Terry's Guide to Mexico*, 1972, p. 162 ff.

*Paz, *The Labyrinth of Solitude*, p. 48.

Jaime Salvador working in the patio of his home in Oaxaca City, constructing the clown (*payaso*) fireworks piece out of reed, papier maché and tissue paper. See color plate for the *payaso* shooting off.

Fireworks-maker Jaime Salvador's four-year-old daughter doing laundry in the patio, Oaxaca.

Salvador's clown fireworks piece finished and fitted with explosives. The tissue paper-covered "wings" at the bottom will make the piece turn as it shoots off. The clown has black crêpe paper hair and beard, a green shirt, black pants and a pasted-on face cut from a magazine. Height 46″, width 21″ (1.17 m. × 53 cm.)

Clown head, detail, showing the face from a magazine that is pasted on, with a built-up nose in the center, and fierce eyebrows painted in black.

The black King, Balthazar riding on a dark gray elephant; all made of papier maché, painted or covered with foil, part of the life-size *nacimiento* of 1967. The Mexican artisan's stylization of the elephant is notable. Height, about 11′ (3.35 m.)

Three Kings riding a horse, an elephant and a camel, led by another Biblical figure in the *nacimiento* in Alameda Park; all figures about life size.

Painted clay *nacimiento* figure—shepherdess with sheep; figures mounted on wires set into a small clay base. When in place in a crêche, the base would disappear under a wealth of Spanish moss. Figure 3½″ tall (8.9 cm.)

Two figures, man and woman market figures with wares, fired pottery painted with tempera colors: brown, white, black, green, red. Very cheap *nacimiento* figures, to be used in crêche scene, with Spanish moss covering the base. Height 3½″ (8.9 cm.)

153

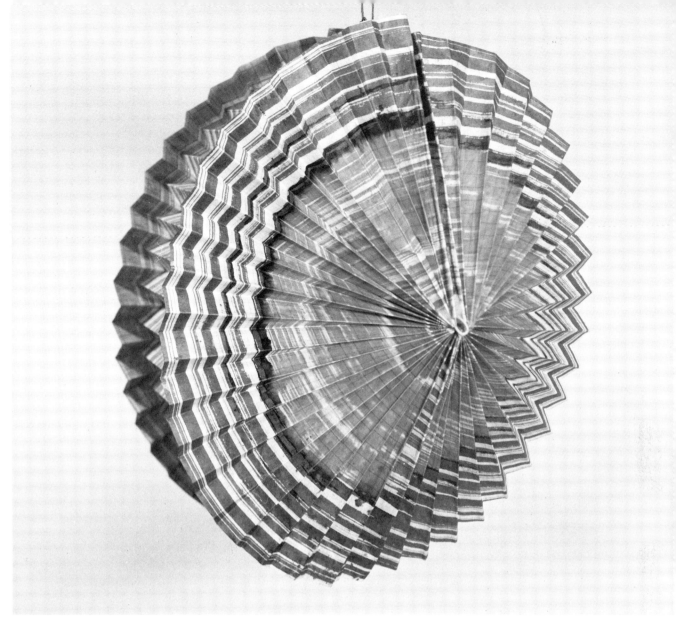

Pleated paper lantern—*farol*—fastened over outdoor lights as a festival decoration; printed in multicolor. Diameter 10″ (25.4 cm.)

Nacimiento in a patio, San Miguel de Allende, Guanajuato, with the customary abundance of Spanish moss.

Opposite page: Red cut tissue paper New Years greeting and magenta foil cut-out Christmas greeting. These decorative papers are sometimes cut individually with scissors, but often they are stamped out twelve or fourteen at a time with die-cutting tools or chisels. 6″ × 4¼″ (15.2 × 10.8 cm.)

Three embossed and painted tin Christmas tree ornaments.
Height 3″ and 4″ (7.6 and 10.2 cm.)

Piglets, pottery painted with aniline colors,
bright pink, white and purple; yellow, blue and
green. Height ⅞″ and 1⅜″ (2.2 and 3.5 cm.)

Opposite page: Two Christmas angels made of natural wheat
straw. Height 4½″ and 5½″ (11.4 and 14 cm.)

Five Christmas ornaments, pottery painted with tempera colors in pastel hues and white. The star is 2½″ across, the gourd is 1½″ (6.4 and 3.8 cm.)

Two flying birds made of natural wheat straw—a very popular hanging Christmas ornament. Wingspreads: 5″ and 9″ (12.7 and 22.9 cm.)

Pottery Christmas ornaments, mold-made and painted with tempera colors and metallic gold. Bells 2″ high, dove 3″ (with wings attached by wires)—(5.1 and 7.6 cm.)

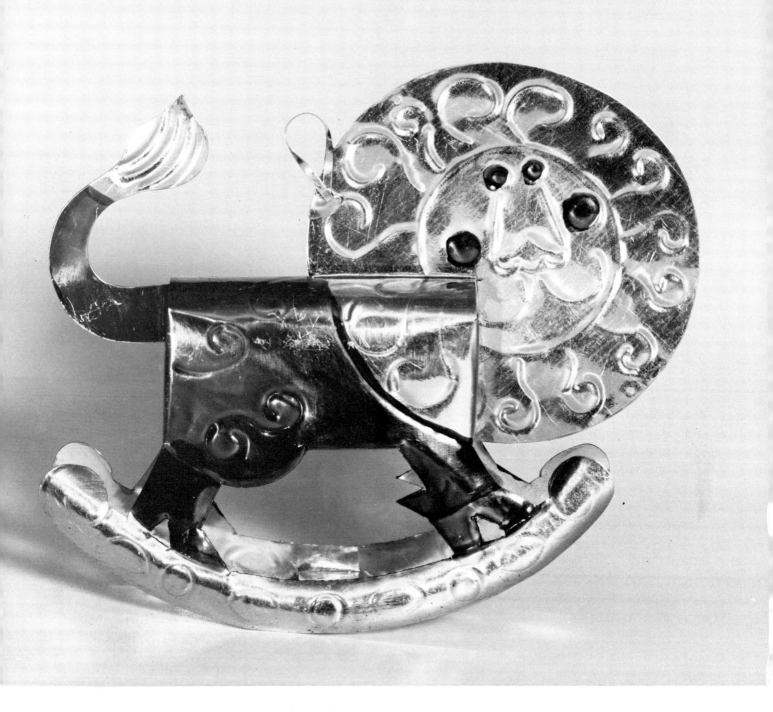

Tin lion, painted with aniline colors; a modern, rather
complicated piece, soldered, and having three dimensions;
colors: red, green and gold. Length 5½″ (14 cm.)

Opposite page: Tin swan, Christmas ornament, with soldered
wings, painted with aniline colors, red, blue, green. Height
5½″ (14 cm.)

Church, painted tin; slightly shaped in a repoussé technique not often practiced in Mexico. Height 5½″ (14 cm.) *Gift of Emily N. Kimball.*

Opposite page: Two unpainted tin Christmas ornaments, rooster and bird; rooster 4″ high, bird 5″ long (10.2 and 12.7 cm.)

Paper lanterns hanging in the zócalo at San Miguel de
Allende, Christmas, 1974.

Christmas display of light constructions decorating the *zócalo*
in Mexico City in 1972. Height of "fountain" 20 feet
(6 metres).

164

Large tissue paper banners flying in the zócalo of Puerto Vallarta, near the church at Christmas time.

Mexico City's magnificent cathedral at one end of the huge, paved zócalo, with flood lights lending it an almost dream-like beauty.

Market at Tlacolula, Oaxaca.

VI

MARKET DAYS, WHERE THINGS ARE MADE, MUSEUMS AND SHOPS

MEXICAN MARKET DAYS – *TIANGUIS*

A listing of some of the more interesting native markets in
Mexico and the days on which the country people and nearby artisans
bring their wares to sell in the "city" markets.*

SUNDAY

Acatlán, Puebla
Cuernavaca, Morelos
Dolores de Hidalgo, Guanajuato
Ixtapan de la Sal, Mexico
Jocotepec, Jalisco
Juchitán, Oaxaca
Morelia, Michoacán
Papantla, Vera Cruz

Puebla, Puebla
San Miguel de Allende, Guanajuato
Taxco, Guerrero
Tehuantepec, Oaxaca
Tenancingo, Mexico
Tequisquiapan, Querétero
Texcoco, Mexico
Tlacolula, Oaxaca
Tonalá, Jalisco
Uruapan, Michoacán

*Norman & Schmidt, page 254

167

Young boy cotton candy vendor, Oaxaca City.

MONDAY

Ixmiquilpan, Hidalgo
Metepec, Mexico

TUESDAY

San Martín Texmelucán, Puebla

THURSDAY & SUNDAY

Morelia, Michoacán

FRIDAY

Ocotlán, Oaxaca
Pátzcuaro, Michoacán
Toluca, Mexico

SATURDAY

Huauchinango, Puebla
Huejotzingo, Puebla
Oaxaca, Oaxaca (principal day)
Tehuacán, Puebla

DAILY

Oaxaca, Oaxaca
San Cristóbal las Casas, Chiapas
Saltillo, Coahuila

Young boy pinwheel vendor, Mexico City, January 1, 1976.

Indian woman carrying milk containers, Oaxaca.

Market at Oaxaca City.

TOYS, HANDCRAFTS, SWEETS AND DECORATIONS*

Listed by the principal places where they are produced

STATE	CITY	PRODUCTS
AGUASCALIENTES	Aguascalientes	Peanut-sprinkled taffy—*charamusca,* twisted into figures and various forms
CHIAPAS	San Cristóbal las Casas	Milk and egg-yolk candies in animal forms; wax figures
GUANAJUATO	Acámbaro	Pottery; loaves of bread 16" in diameter for festivals
	Celaya	Papier mâché masks, skulls, carnival heads made in three districts: Tierras Negras, Zapote and San Juan; *alfeñique* sugar paste candy; pottery
	Guanajuato	Papier mâché toys and dolls, tissue paper banners; scenes in nutshells that open
	Irapuato	Pottery; cut tissue paper banners
	Salamanca	Puppets; wooden toys
	San Miguel de Allende	Fine *Alfeñique;* papier mâché; *piñatas;* painted tin ornaments
	Santa Cruz	Wire-reenforced papier mâché toys: dolls, skeletons on horseback, witches, hairy spiders. Painted clay household miniatures, trees of life, *nacimiento* figures and *arrocitos* by Demetrio Ramirez
	Silao	Wood miniatures: kitchen cupboards, shelves; jumping jacks, boxers, springing tigers, crocodiles; pottery
	Yuríria	Pottery; cut tissue paper banners
	State-wide	Pottery centers: Guanajuato, Coroneo, Dolores Hidalgo, San Luis de la Paz, Acámbaro, Irapuato, San Diego de la Unión, Ciudad Manuel Doblado, San Felipe Torresmochas, Celaya, Silao, Yuríria, Salvatierra & Jerécuaro

*Material in this section is taken in part from: *El Juguete Mexicano* by Tonatiuh and Elektra Gutierrez

GUERRERO	Ameyaltepec	Painted clay figures and animals
	Olinalá	Lacquer work, masks for tiger dance; famous mask-maker: Ismael Garcia
	Taxco	Silver and silver jewelry
	Teloloapan	Clay toys for Corpus Christi, made and fired by children
	State-wide	Pottery centers: San Miguel Huapan, San Augustín de las Flores, Toliman, Xalita, Zumpango. Ivory-colored ware painted with dark animals and flowers
	Iguala, Toliman, Xalita, Ameyaltepec, San Augustín de las Flores	Tempera painting on brown *amate* bark paper in the style of Guerrero pottery in bright colors
HIDALGO	Ixmiquilpan	Reed (*carrizo*) flutes, serpents, tiny baskets (*aguinaldos*) toy musical instruments made by Otomí Indians; abalone inlays
	Valle de Mezquital	Miniature musical instruments, chess and domino sets with abalone inlay by the Pedraza family; palm leaf rattles in bird forms with feather tails
JALISCO	Guadalajara	Hand blown glass, glass miniatures by Odilón Avalos; rag dolls; Palm Sunday palm ornaments
	Santa Ana Acatlán	Pottery piggy banks with dull black finish, painted with floral motifs and varnished; whistles, animals, jumping jacks; clay toys by Julian Acero and Candelario Medrano
	Talpa de Allende	Chicle miniatures: toys, sculptures, flower baskets, vases, saints, crucifixes, bird cages
	Teocaltiche	Turned wooden toys: tops, cup and ball, yo-yos, chessmen; dice
	Tlaquepaque	Pottery toys made in molds by the Panduras family: "caricature fruits" with priests, clowns, policemen, etc.
	Tonalá	Famous pottery by Jorge Wilmot; miniature glazed dishes, burnished ware; miniature kitchenware by Doña Celsa Medrano; *barro de olor* by Almado Galván
	Zapopán	Huichol votive objects: *ojo de dios, nearikas* and *chaquiras*
	State-wide	Pottery centers: Tatepozco, Salatitan, San Martín de las Flores, Tonalá, Coyula and San Gaspar

MEXICO	Ixtapan	Wood carvings from white wood, especially mice.
	Lerma	*Tule* reed figures, especially horsemen of the Revolution (*carranclanes*)
	Metepec	Black glazed pottery animals, toys, banks; red clay tree of life
	Mexico, D. F.	Papier mâché and cardboard Judases, skeletons, clowns, demons, masks, hats, helmets, *alebrijes* and *piñatas* by Pedro Linares and family; miniature metal tea sets
	Toluca	Fine *alfeñique;* miniature furniture; *matracas;* baskets; chess sets, and dominoes of horn, bone and wood; wax candles
	Valle de Brava	Pottery
MICHOACAN	Capula	Pottery; toys
	Michoacán	Toy trains, airplanes, ferris wheels, bicycles, *charros,* bird cages—all made of various fibers: cane, reed, *ixtle, lechugilla,* rush, *maguey* and wheat straw
	Morelia	Rag dolls
	Ocumicho	Glazed, polychrome ceramics: devils, beasts, dogs, wolves, serpents
	Paracho	Sugar-water "fruit" candy packed in scrap-wood boxes; miniature guitars and violins with abalone inlay
	Pátzcuaro	Fine lacquer work; straw objects
	Quiroga	Lacquer work; pottery
	Santa Clara del Cobre	Copper, copper miniatures of all kinds
	Santa Fe	Pottery
	Tzintzuntzán	*Tule* and wheat straw airplanes, animals, angels, crucifixions, Virgins and *nacimiento* figures
	Uruapan	Lacquer work
	Villa Morelos	Pottery toys
	State-wide	Pottery centers: Comanjá, Zacapú, Ario, Huandacareo, Santo Tomás, Zinapecuaro
OAXACA	Arrasola	Carved and painted wood figures, animals, *nacimientos* by Manuel Jiménez
	Jamiltepec	Pottery: pre-Hispanic turtle rattles, small animals and figures
	Juchitán de Zaragoza	Pottery female figures (*tanguyus*) painted white with bright color decoration; pottery houses, horses, and black pottery

OAXACA	Ocotlán	Pottery center: bells in form of long-skirted women, baptismal and wedding scenes; *nacimientos;* painted pottery by the Aguilar family; incense burners
	San Bartólo Coyotepec	Pottery center—famous for unglazed, burnished black pottery by Doña Rosa; bells, figures, whistles, vases, jars, sieves, lanterns, beads
	Santa María Atzompa	Pottery center; dark buff clay partly or entirely unglazed; dark green glaze only; toys, miniatures, whistles, animals for *chia* seeds, *ollas.* Most famous potter: Teodora Blanco
	Tehuantepec	Pottery—small clay dolls with tempera decoration
PUEBLA	Acatlán	Pottery—black or red vessels and piggy banks with white decoration; polychromed *barro de olor* by Herón Martinez—also tree of life, masks, amusing animals
	Cholula	Tissue paper cut-out banners
	Huaquechula	Candle holders and pottery painted figures for the Day of the Dead and Christmas
	Izucar de Matamoros	Traditional small pottery horses and figures painted with tempera and varnished; tree of life by Aurelio Flores and the Castillo brothers
	Puebla	Pottery center; Talavera ceramics and tiles; hand-decorated wax candles; pressed glass; altars for the Day of the Dead made of wood and paper with sugar paste skulls, bread, fruit and vegetables
	San Andres Huixcolotla	Tissue paper cut-outs and foil flowers by the Vivanco family
	San Pablito	*Amate* bark paper made by Otomís
	Santa Maria Chimecatitlán	Palm leaf figures
	Tehuacán	Tissue paper cutouts
	Texmelucan	Tissue paper cut-outs
	Zacapoaxtla	Tissue paper cut-outs
QUERETARO	Querétaro	Wooden doll house furniture; tiny leather saddles and sandals
SAN LUIS POTOSI	San Luis Potosi	Corn shuck *mulitos;* rabbit fur monkeys

TABASCO	Tenosique	Chicle animals, fruit, etc.
VERA CRUZ	Huatusco	Pottery: toy horsemen and dolls
	Papantla	Vanilla bean miniatures
YUCATAN	Campeche	Vanilla bean miniatures; carved tortoise shell
	Mérida	*Piñatas,* paper flowers, birds

Market at Ocotlán, Oaxaca.

FOLK ART MUSEUMS AND SHOPS

Folk Art Museum-Shops sponsored by the Mexican Government

Mexico City
    Arte Popular de Guerrero
    Paseo de la Reforma No. 8
    Esq. Bucareli

    Exposicion Nacional de Arte Popular
    Av. Juarez No. 89

    Salon de Artesanias de Michoacán
    Glorieta Metro Insurgentes Local 14

    Exposicion Turistico Artesanal
    Av. Juarez No. 92 (BANFOCO)

    Museo de Artes e Industrias Populares
    Av. Juarez No. 44

Ciudad Juarez, Chihuahua
    Centro Artesanal Ciudad Juarez
    Anillo Envolvente Lincoln y Mejia

Ensenada, Baja California
    Centro Artesanal Ensenada
    Av. Lopez Mateos No. 1306
    Construcciones Pronaf

La Paz, Baja California
    Centro Artesanal La Paz
    Parque Cuauhtemoc entre Bravo y Rosales

Matamoros, Tamaulipas
    Centro Artesanal Matamoros
    Calle 5a. Iturbide y Alvaro Obregon
Nuevo Laredo, Tamaualipas
    Centro Artesanal Nuevo Laredo
    Maclovio Herrera No. 3030

Piedras Negras, Coahuila
    Centro Artesanal Piedras Negras
    Edificio La Estrella Puerta Mexico

Puebla, Puebla
    Tienda Covento Santa Rosa—Puebla
    Calle 3 Norte No. 1203

Tlaquepaque, Jalisco
    Av. Juarez No. 267—B

Museums

    Museo Regional de Oaxaca
    Avenida Independencia
    Oaxaca

    Museo de Artes Populares
    Toluca, Mexico

    Museo Bello
    Avenida 3 Poniente 302
    Puebla, Puebla

    El Museo del Estado de Jalisco
    Guadalajara, Jalisco

    Museo de San Luis Potosi
    San Luis Potosi

    El Alhondiga de Granaditas
    Guanajuato, Guanajuato

    Museo Nacional de Antropología
    Chapultepec Park
    Mexico, D. F.

    Museo del Arte Popular
    Plaza Grande
    Pátzcuaro, Michoacán

    Museum of the American Indian
    Broadway at 155th Street
    New York, N. Y.

    The American Museum of Natural History
    Central Park West at 79th Street
    New York, N. Y.

    The Field Museum of Natural History
    Chicago, Illinois

Museum of Craft and Folk Art
5814 Wilshire Boulevard
Los Angeles, California 90036

Los Angeles Museum of Natural History
Exposition Park
Los Angeles, California

Mingei International Museum of World Folk Art
University Towne Centre
4405 La Jolla Village Drive
La Jolla, California 92038

Markets

Nuevo Mercado Libertad
Calzada Independencia y
Avenida Juarez
Guadalajara, Jalisco

Mercado de Artes Populares
Calles Dolores y Ayuntamiento
Mexico, D. F.

Bazar Sabado (Saturday Bazaar)
Plaza San Jacinto No. 11
San Angel
Mexico, D. F.

Shops

NOTE: This list is by no means complete, and does not
constitute an endorsement of the shops listed

OAXACA
Jarceria—el Arte Oaxaqueño
Esquina Mina y J. P. Garcia
(West end of the public market)

Productos Tipicos de Oaxaca
Av. Dr. B Dominquez No. 602

Victor—Artes Regionales
Profirio Diaz No. 111

Zen-Mar
Profirio Diaz No. 103

Casa Bustamente
Avenida Independencia

Yalálag
M. Alcalá No. 104

GUANAJUATO, GTO.
Casa de Artesanias
Parque Las Embajadores

SAN MIGUEL DE ALLENDE, GTO.
Casa Isa
Portal, el zócalo

Casa Anguiano
Calle de Canal No. 9

Casa Maxwell
Casa de Canal No. 14

Artes de Mexico
(1) Calzada Aurora No. 49
(2) Esquina Zacateros y Codo

GUADALAJARA, JALISCO
Casa de las Artesanias de Jalisco
5 de febrero

TLAQUEPAQUE, JALISCO
Aldana, S. A.
Progreso 40

TONALA, JALISCO
Aldana, S. A.
Avenida Tonalá 57

ZAPOPAN, JALISCO
Church of the Virgin of Zapopán
(The church sponsors a small
shop that sells Huichol Indian
artifacts and ritual objects)

MEXICO, D. F.
Victor
Artes Populares Mexicanas
Madero No. 10—Rm. 305

THE UNITED STATES
Mexican Folk Art Annex
23 W. 56th Street
New York, N. Y.

Artes de Mexico
Bazar del Mundo
Old Town State Park
San Diego, California

VII

GLOSSARY

SPANISH-ENGLISH

A

abulón—abalone shell
adorno—decoration, ornament
aguila—eagle
aguinaldo—small basket; Christmas or New Years gift
alambre—wire
alebrije—fantastic animal
alcancia—bank (money box)
alfarería—pottery
alfarero (a)—potter
alfeñique—sugar-paste candy
amate (amatl)—bark paper
angelito—little angel
arbol de la vida—tree of life
arrocito (arrocillos)—"rice toys", miniatures
artesano—artisan
atl—Aztec word for water

B

balero—cup and ball toy
balón—balloon
barrio—neighborhood or district
barro—clay
barro bandero—"flag" pottery
barro de olor—a fragrant, burnished ochre ware pottery from Tonalá

baston—cane (walking stick)
batea—lacquered wood tray
bateitas—miniature lacquer trays
bolsa—bag
bordadero—embroidery
brasero—brazier; charcoal stove
bruja—witch
brujo—warlock (male witch)
brujería—witchcraft
bruñido—burnished
burrito—little burro
burro—small donkey, burro
buscapies—crackling fireworks

C

calavera—skull; printed broadside
canasta—basket
canastilla—little basket
candela—candle
carretita—little cart
carrita—cart
carrizo—bamboo; also reed and grass figures
carroza—carriage
carusel—carrousel
cartón—cardboard, corrugated board
casco—helmet
castillo—"castle" of fireworks

cera—wax
ceramica—ceramic ware; pottery
cerdito de barro—clay pig
cesta—basket
chango—monkey
chaquira—gourd with glass bead lining (Huichol Indian)
charamusca—taffy
charro—Mexican cowboy
chichihuites—willow basketry
cobre—copper
cochinita de alcancia—piggy bank
cohetes—small fireworks
cohetero—fireworks-maker
conejo—rabbit
comal—flat pottery griddle for cooking tortillas
copal—tree used for wood carving & incense
corona—crown
corrida—romance (novel)
criollo—person of pure Spanish blood living in the
    Americas
cruz—cross
cuero—leather
curandero—folk doctor

D

día de fiesta—holiday
día festivo—holiday
diablillo—little devil
diablo—devil
diábolo—wood and string toy
dorado—gilded
dulces—sweets, candies

E

esqueleto—skeleton
estambre—wool yarn

F

feria—fair, festival
festividad—festivity, merry-making
festivola—gay, festive, joyful
fiesta—feast, celebration, day of merriment
fiesta de pólvora—fireworks celebration
fuego—fire

G

gallo—cook, rooster
globo—balloon

H

huaraches—leather sandals
hechicería—witchcraft
hoja de lata—tin plate
hoja de maiz—corn shuck or husk
hueso—bone

I

ixtle—cactus-like plant used for its fiber

J

jaula—cage
jícara—gourd bowl
jicarita—small chocolate cup
Judas—large figure with fireworks
juguete—toy
juguetería—toy shop
juego—game

L

laca—lacquer
lata—tin
"ladinos"—citified people
labrillo—glazed earthenware tub
loza—chinaware

M

machete—heavy chopping knife
maguey—common cactus-like plant
marfil—ivory
maromero—acrobat, jumping jack
martillado—hammered
máscara—mask
matraca—whirling noisemaker
meco—"wild" Indian puppet
mestizo—person of mixed Spanish and Indian blood
mimbre—reed, rattan
misterios—*nacimiento* figures (crèche)
molcajete—mortar (for grinding)
molde—mold, as of clay or plaster
molinillo—wooden chocolate beater
monigote—puppet
muchacho, muchacha—boy, girl
mueblecitos—miniature furniture
muertos—the dead
mulito—little mule
mulo—mule
muñeca—doll
muñeca de trapo—rag doll
musiquitos—little musicians

N

nacimiento—Christmas crèche or Nativity scene
nealíka—god-disc (Huichol Indian)
nearíka—wool yarn votive tablet or *tablillo* (Huichol
    Indian)
nueces—nuts
nuez—nut, nutshell

O

ofrenda—altar offering

ojo de dios—eye of god—wool yarn votive symbol (Huichol Indian)
olla—round clay cooking pot used also for making *piñatas*
ollita—small pot

P

paja—straw
pan, panes—bread, breads
panicua—wheat straw
pantalones—pants
papalote—kite
papel machado, pegado, prensado—papier mâché
papel picado—paper cut-out
pasta de azucar—sugar-paste candy
pastillaje—applied clay ornament on clay objects
payaso—clown
payaso de fuelle—clown on a stick with bellows that squeak
pelea de gallos—cockfight
pelele—scarecrow
penitentes—religious penitents
pepitas—seeds used in rattles
pequeñito—teeny weeny thing
perinolas—dice
petate—all-purpose reed or palm mat
petatillo—decorated ceramic ware
picante—highly seasoned, spicy
piel—skin, hide, leather
piñata—decorated clay pot for Christmas season game
pincel—brush
pirotécnicas—large fireworks
pirotécnico—master fireworks maker
platito—little plate
plato—plate
plumas—feathers
plomo—lead
pólvora—fireworks
popote—broomstraw
posada—Christmas procession
pueblo—village; people
puesto—stand or market stall
pulque—cheap liquor made from the maguey plant
punto de cruz—cross stitch

Q

quexquémetl—shoulder cape

R

rebozo—long scarf-head covering
rehilete—pinwheel
rueda de fortuna—ferris wheel; wheel of fortune

S

sahumador—incense burner

serpiente—snake
shaman—chief magician
silbato—whistle
sonaja—rattle
sonajeros—dancers with rattles

T

tablillo de estambre—wood plaque with wool design (Huichol Indian)
tamale—ground meat wrapped in corn meal and steamed in corn husks
talla, tallado—carved work
tanguyús—small New Years and betrothal toys made of clay, painted
tecolete—owl
tejamanil—scrap wood used for toy-making—shingle
temple—tempera paint
tianguis—market day
titero—puppet
torito pirotécnico—little bull with fireworks
toro—bull
tortilla—flat corn cake
trastecito—miniature kitchen cupboard
trapo—rag
trastero—cupboard
trazo—design
trigo—wheat
trompo—top; chessman
trompón—very large top
tule—rush or reed

V

vela—candle
vidriada—glazed (as pottery)
vidrio—glass
vidrio soplado—blown glass
viejitos—little old men
volantín—flying swing or merry-go-round

X

xalama—tree for black bark paper-making
xochitl—Aztec word for flower

Y

yerma—egg-yolk candy
yeso—plaster

Z

zempasúchitl—marigold-like flower of the dead
zócalo—the central square of Mexican towns and cities; sometimes a paved plaza bordered by a cathedral and government buildings; sometimes a central park and gathering place

ENGLISH-SPANISH

A

abalone shell—abulon
acrobat—maromero
amate bark paper—papel amate
artisan—artesano

B

bag—bolsa
balloon—balón; globo
bamboo—bambú; carrizo
bank—alcancia (money box)
bark paper—amate, amatl
basket—canasta; cesta, canastilla
basket, small—aguinaldo
bone—hueso
boy—muchacho
brazier—brasero
bread, breads—pan, panes
broomstraw—popote
brush—pincel
bull (little)—torito
bull—toro
bull with fireworks—torito pirotécnico
burnished—bruñido
burro (little)—burrito

C

cage—jaula
candies—dulces
candle—vela; candela
cane (walking stick)—bastón
cardboard—cartón
carousel—carusel
cart—carroza, carrota, carretita
carved work—talla; tallado
"castle" of fireworks—castillo
censer—sahumador
ceramic ware—ceramica
charcoal stove—brasero
chessman—trompo
chinaware—loza
chocolate beater—molinillo
citified people—ladinos
clay pig—cerdito de barro
clay—barro
clown—payaso
cock—gallo
cock-fight—pelea de gallos
corn cake—tortilla
corn husks or shucks—hoja de maiz
cowboy (Mexican)—charro
crèche—nacimiento

crèche figures—misterios
cross—cruz
cross-stitch—punto de cruz
crown—corona
cup and ball toy—balero
cupboard—trastero

D

dead (the)—muertos
decoration—adorno
design—trazo
devil—diablo
doll—muñeca
diabolo—diabolo (toy)
dice—perinolas

E

eagle—aguila
egg-yolk candy—yerma
embroidered—bordado
embroidery—bordadero
eye of god—ojo de dios

F

fair—feria
fantastic animal—alebrije
feathers—plumas
ferris wheel—rueda de fortuna
festival—feria
finery—adorno
fire—fuego
fireworks—cohetes, pirotécnicas, pólvora
fireworks-maker—cohetero, pirotécnico
fireworks celebration—fiesta de pólvora
"flag" pottery—barro bandero
flying swing—volantín
folk doctor—curandero
furniture (miniature)—mueblecitos

G

game—juego
gift—regalo, aguinaldo
gilded—dorado
girl—muchacha
glass—vidrio
glass, blown—vidrio soplado
glazed—vidriada
god-disc—nealíka (Huichol Indian)
gourd bowl—jicara
gourd bowl with glass bead decoration—chaquira
(Huichol Indian)

H

hammered—martillado
helmet—casco
hide, leather—piel, cuero
holiday—día festivo; día de fiesta

I

incense burner—sahumador
Indian ("wild")—meco
ivory—marfil

J

Judas—figura con cohetes
jumping jack (acrobat)—maromero

K

kite—papalote
kitchenware (miniature)—trastecitos
knife, heavy chopping—machete

L

lacquer—laca
lacquered tray—batea
lead—plomo
leather—cuero, piel

M

marigold—zempasúchitl—(Indian flower of the dead)
market day—tianguis
mask—máscara
masked "black" dancers—negritos
mat of reed or palm—petate
melon seeds—pepitas
merry-go-round—volantín
monkey—chango
mold—molde
mortar (for grinding)—molcajete
mule—mulo, mulito

N

neighborhood—barrio
noisemaker—matraca
nut or nutshell—nuez
nuts—nueces

O

offering (altar)—ofrenda
ornament—adorno
owl—tecolete

P

paint brush—pincel
paper cut-out—papel picado

papier mâché—cartón, papel machado, papel pegado, papel prensado
people—pueblo
piggy bank—cochinita de alcancia
pinwheel—rehilete
plaster—yeso
plate—plato, platito
pot (cooking or for a piñata)—olla
potter—alfarero (a)
pottery—alfarería
puppet—titere, monigote
puppet with feathers—meco

R

rabbit—conejo
rag—trapo
rag doll—muñeca de trapo
rattan (reed)—mimbre
rattle—sonaja
reed and grass figures—carrizo
repoussé (French)—shaping metal by hammering
rice toys—arrocitos, arrocillos
romance (novel)—corrida
rooster—gallo
rush—tule

S

sandals (leather)—huaraches
scarecrow—pelele
seeds for rattles—pepitas
skeleton—esqueleto
skin—piel
skull—calavera
snake—serpiente
straw—paja
sugar-paste candy—alfeñique
sweets (candies)—dulces

T

tablet of wool yarn—nearíka; tablillo de estambre
tempera paint—temple
tight rope walker (jumping jack)—maromero
tin—lata
tin-plate—hoja de lata
Tonalá clay ware—petatillo
top—trompo
top (large)—trompón
toy—juguete
toy shop—juguetería
tree of life—arbol de la vida
tub—labrillo

V

village—pueblo
votive bowl—chaquira (Huichol Indian)
votive tablet—nearíka (Huichol Indian)

W

warlock (male witch)—brujo
wax—cera
wheat—trigo
wheat straw—panicua, paja de trigo
whistle—silbato

willow basketry—chichihuites
wire—alambre
witch—bruja
witchcraft—brujería, hechicería
wood (scrap)—tejamanil
wool yarn—estambre

VIII

BIBLIOGRAPHY

Atl, Dr. See Murillo

Berdecio, Robert and Appelbaum, Sidney (Eds.) *Posada's Popular Mexican Prints.* New York: Dover Publications Inc., 1972

Brenner, Anita. *Idols Behind Altars.* Payson, 1929

Calderon de la Barca, Frances E. *Life in Mexico During a Residence of Two Years in That Country.* New York: Dutton, 1931

Christensen, Bodil and Marti, Samuel. *Brujerías y papel precolombino.* (Witchcraft and Pre-Columbian Paper.) Mexico, D. F.: Ediciones Euroamericanas, Klaus Thiele, 1972

Codex Mendoza, The. Written by native scribes for viceroy Don Antonio de Mendoza (1535-1550.) Bodleian Library, Oxford, England: edited by James Cooper Clark, London, Waterlow and Sons, 1938

Dockstader, Frederick J. *Indian Art in Middle America.* Greenwich, Connecticut: N. Y. Graphic Society Publishers, Ltd., 1964

Dörner, Gerd. *Folk Art of Mexico.* New York: A. S. Barnes & Co., 1962

El Juguete Mexicano. Mexico, D. F.: Artes de Mexico; año XVI, No. 125, 1969

Espejel, Carlos. *Las Artesanías Tradicionales en Mexico.* Sep/Setentas; Secretaría de Educación Publica: Mexico, D. F., 1972

Girard, Alexander. *The Magic of a People.* A Studio Book; New York: The Viking Press, 1968

Grove, Richard. *Mexican Popular Arts Today.* Colorado Springs, Colo.: The Taylor Museum of the Colorado Springs Fine Arts Center, 1954

Gutierrez, Tonatiúh y Elektra. *El Arte Popular de Mexico.* Mexico, D. F.: Artes de Mexico, Numero Extraordinario, 1970-1971

Lannik, William, Palm, R. L. and Takton, Marsha P. *Paper Figures and Folk Medicine among the San Pablito Otomí.* Indian Notes and Monographs #57. New York: Museum of the American Indian Heye Foundation, 1969

Lewis, Oscar. *Five Families.* New York: Basic Books, 1959

———— *The Children of Sanchez.* N. Y.: Random House, 1961

———— *A Death in the Sanchez Family.* N. Y.: Random House, 1969

Lo Efímero y Eterno del Arte Popular Mexicana. Tomo I; Fondo Editorial de las Plástica Mexicana: Mexico, D. F.: Banco Nacional de Comercio Exterior, S. A., 1971

Mitos, Ritos y Hechicerías. Mexico, D. F.: Artes de Mexico, año XVI, No. 124, 1969

Murillo, Gerardo (Dr. Atl). *Las Artes Populares en Mexico* Ed. Cultura—Secretaria de Industria y Comercio, 1922

Museo Nacional de Antropología. Mexico, D. F.: Artes de Mexico, año XVI, No. 125, 1969

Nacimiento, Villancico y Pastorela. Mexico, D. F.: Artes de Mexico, No. 262, 1960

Norman, James and Schmidt, Margaret Fox. *A Shopper's Guide to Mexico.* A Dolphin Handbook #C 466. Garden City, N. Y.: Doubleday & Co., Inc. 1973

Norman, James. *Terry's Guide to Mexico.* Garden City, N. Y.: Doubleday & Co., Inc. Use latest revision.

Paalen, Isabel de Marin. *Arte de Mexicano Etno Artesanías y Arte Popular.* Mexico, D. F.: Editorial Hermes, 1974

Rivera, Diego and Wolfe, B. D. *Portrait of Mexico.* B. Y. Covici Friede, 1937

Rubin, de la Borbolla, Daniel. *Las Artes Populares Guanajuatenses,* 1961

——— *Arte Popular y Artesanías de Mexico.* Mexico, D. F. Nos. 43/44, 11th year

Soustelle, Jacques. *Mexico—Archeología Mundi.* Cleveland and New York: World Publishing Co., Inc. 1967

——— *Daily Life of the Aztecs on the Eve of the Spanish Conquest,* Stanford University Press, Stanford, California, 1970. Originally published by Hachette, Paris, 1955 as: *La vie quotidienne des aztèques à la veille de la conquète espagnole*

Terry's Guide to Mexico—see Norman

Toneyama, Kojin. *The Popular Arts of Mexico.* N. Y. and Tokyo: Weatherhill/Heibonsha, 1974

Toor, Frances. *A Treasury of Mexican Folkways.* New York: Crown Publishers, Inc., 1947

——— *Mexican Popular Arts.* Mexico, D. F.: Frances Toor Studios, 1939. Republished, 1973 by Blaine Ethridge Books, Detroit, Michigan

Vazquez, Pedro Ramirez. *The National Museum of Anthropology of Mexico.* New York: Harry Abrams, Inc., in association with Helvetica Press, Inc., 1968

NOTES ON THE PHOTOGRAPHY

All scenes and objects photographed in Mexico were done with 35 mm single-lens reflex cameras with interchangeable lenses. The lenses used were 50 mm f/1.9, 50 mm f/2.8, 50 mm macro, 55 mm f/1.8, 28 mm f/4, 85 mm f/4 and 135 mm f/4. The films used were Kodacolor II (ASA 80), Plus X (ASA 125) and Tri X (ASA 400). Accessories used were: a cable release, exposure meter (to complement those in the cameras), neutral test card, automatic electronic flash and a small tripod. A white window shade was used as a reflector, and at times as a background. Various colors of wrapping paper bought in Mexico were also used as backgrounds when required. The Kodacolor film was used to photograph scenes and objects outdoors in sunlight. The electronic flash was used indoors when there was insufficient available light. Both black & white prints and 4 × 5 Ektacolor print film transparencies were made from these negatives. The Plus X film was used in sunlight to photograph objects. The Tri X film was used to photograph children in sunlight from a distance, usually with the 135 mm lens. The same film was used indoors with flash to take people at work and also indoors under available light to photograph museum objects when flash was not permitted. The films (Plus X and Tri X) produced black & white prints only.

Many objects were sent from Mexico to our home in the States to be photographed. One end of our living room was our photographic studio with a table, boxes, background materials of seamless paper and colored poster boards, spotlights and reflectors and light stands. 500 and 250 watt 3200° Kelvin lamps were used. The photographs done in the studio were made with a 4 × 5 view camera using either a 162 mm (6⅜″) or a 25 cm (10″) lens and Royal Pan (ASA 400) film for black & white photos and Ektachrome type B for 4 × 5 transparencies. Accessories used were a large tripod, exposure meter, neutral test card and a cable release.

Four photographs were copied from a Mexican book (with the permission of the publisher—Editorial Hermes, S.A.) using a view camera with 4 × 5 Professional Copy film to produce black & white prints.

R M P

CREDITS

The author and the photographer extend their sincere thanks
to the following for granting the privilege of photographing
or making use of their material to illustrate this book:

Jean and Russell Ames of Etla, Oaxaca, Stephen and Yvonne Forbath of Guadalajara, Jalisco, Mrs. Walter W. Frese of Stamford, Connecticut, Emily N. Kimball of Newtown, Connecticut and Carlos Espejel, former director of The Museum of Popular Arts and Industries, Mexico City.

Illustrations on page 48, 49 (top), 56 (top left), 122 and 123 were photographed in the museum-shop BANFOCO (*Fideicomiso para el Fomento de las Artesanías,* Mexico City.

Illustrations on pages 129 (bottom), 130 (upper left), 77, 78 and 95 (bottom) were photographed at the Regional Museum, Oaxaca City.

Prints on pages 120 (upper right) and 134 are courtesy of Dover Publications; from *Posada's Popular Mexican Prints* by Berdecio and Appelbaum.

The woodcut on page 116 is by Robert Montenegro, illustrating the Carnival of Zaachila, Oaxaca; courtesy of *Mexican Folkways.*

The engraving on page 139 (top) is from *Mexican Folkways,* Vol. 4, No. 4; October-December, 1928, page 241.

The engraving on page 146 (top) is from *Mexican Folkways,* Vol. 3. No. 1; February-March, 1927, page 79.

Drawings on pages 13, 14, 73 and 75 were made by the author from material in The American Museum of Natural History, New York, N. Y.

The drawing on page 76 was made by the author from material in the Museum of the American Indian, Heye Foundation, New York, N. Y.

The photographs on pages 125 (top) and 145 (top) are courtesy of the Mexican National Tourist Council, New York, N. Y.

Photographs on page 73 (right), 75 (upper right) and 97 (bottom right) are courtesy of the Mexican Chamber of Commerce of the United States, New York, N. Y.

Photographs on pages 66, 67, 70 and 131 (bottom) are courtesy of Editorial Hermes, S. A., Mexico, D. F.; from *Etno Artesanías y Arte Popular Mexicano,* pages 170, 172 and 174.

INDEX

Principal references are shown in **bold face** numerals

A

abalone shell 79
Acapulco 125
Acatlán, Puebla 87
aerial balloons 99
affairs of love and hate 71
Aguascalientes City 123
Alameda Park, Mexico City 114
alborada 111
alfeñique 92, 129, 131
All Saints' Day 128
All Souls' Day 128
Altar of Sorrows 117
altars 70
amate bark paper 66-67, 70, 80
amatl 66
Andalusia 35
aniline colors 81, 98
aplicado lacquer 93
artifacts, fake 88
Ash Wednesday 115-116, 118
Atl, Dr. 16-17
Atzompa—see Santa María Atzompa
August events 127
Aztecs 17, 65, 71, 139

B

Balthazar 114
bamboo 103
bark paper 66
Battle of Moors and Christians 126
Battle of Puebla 124
beads 82
bed, *amate* paper 70
beeswax 82, 107
Bethlehem 114, 139
boar bristles 82
Bonampak 12
bread of the dead 129, 131
broomstraws 83
bruja, brujo 67, 69
brujería 71
buñuelos 144
burnishing clay 89

C

calaveras 132, 135
Calderon, Fanny 140
calendar of events 111

Campeche, Tampico 115
Candelmas Day 115
candles 67, 70-71, 108, 112
cane 103
carnival costumes 95
carrizo 97
castillos 103, 112, 123, 138, **146-148**
Cathedral, Mexico City 125
Catherine wheels 146
Catholic churches 65, 71
Catholicism 65
Celaya, Guanajuato 102, 117
chants, ceremonial 70
Chapultepec Park, Mexico City 127
chaquira 82
charamusca 117
Chiapas 66, 77
chia seeds 83-84
chickens 67, 70
chickpeas 85
chicle 85
chiclets 85
children as potters 88
Chimulas 77
China paper 69
Christmas 145
    celebrations 145
    sweets and decorations 144
churches 65, 112
    Santa Prisca, Taxco 118, 143
    Soledad, Oaxaca 139
Ciudad del Carmen, Campeche 126
clay 86
    burnishing 89
    children as potters 88
    decorations 87
    firing 87
    mold-casting 86
    pottery villages 88
    shaping 86
    surface textures 87
clown (*payaso*) fireworks 149
codices 14, 66
cohetero 145
copal, copalillo 109
copper 89
Coras 66, 76
corn 90
cornshuck dolls 90
cornshucks 90
Corpus Christi 90, 98, 107, 112, 125
Cortes, Hernando 13

costumbre, the 69-70
    of the Well 70
cotton 90
Coyoacan, D. F. 126
Coyótepec—see San Bartólo Coyotepec
crêpe paper 99
crucifixion 118

D

dance of *los Moros* 126
    los Negritos 95
    los Viejitos 95
    the Reed Throwers 71
    the Tigers 82
Day of the Dead 85, 90, 108, 112, **128**
    customs 131
    flower 131
    foods 129
    Indian ceremonies 136
Day of the Three Kings 112-114, 144
December events 137
decoration of clay pieces 87
deities 69, 72
día de la Candelaría 114
d'Harnoncourt, René 15
dolls, cornshuck 90
    fireworks piece 149
    Flower of Heaven 70
    Guardian of the Door 70
    paper **67,** 69-71
don Juan Tenorio 135
dorado lacquer 93
Durango 116

E

Eames, Charles 11
Easter 112, 117
eggs 70
el Alhondiga museum 131, 150
el día de la Raza 127
el día de San Isidro 124
el Grito 127
el Pelele 123
embrutido lacquer 93
Empress Carlotta 116
encrustado lacquer 93
Epiphany 113-114
Etla, Oaxaca 116, 123
Eye of God 74

F

face painting 72, 76
fake artifacts 88
Feast of *San José* 116
    San Ramón 127
    the Assumption 127
    the Holy Innocents 145
    the Immaculate Conception 137-138
Feather Dance 91, 114, 126
feathers 74, 91
February events 115
ferris wheel 108
Fiesta de la Virgen de Salud 138
fiestas 111, 124-127, 143, 146
fireworks 111, 117, **145-150**
firing pottery 87
Flag Day 115
flowers 70, 74, 91, 99
    of the Dead 131
Flying Pole Dance 71, 107, 125
foil paper 99
folk arts 17-18, 36
    museums and shops 35, **173**
food offerings 74
foods, Day of the Dead 129
fuegos artificiales 111, **145-150**

G

glass 92
glitter, metallic 92
Good Friday 121
gourds 92
Grove, Richard 18
Guadalajara, Jalisco 92
Guanajuato 96
Guatemala 85, 91
Guerrero 80, 95
guitar 75
    covered with broomstraws 83

H

henequen 91
herbes 67
Hernandez, Francisco Javier 14
Hidalgo, Padre 127
Holy Cross, Feast of the 124
Holy Week 112, 117, 118
huaraches 94

Huehuetla, Puebla 107
Huejotzingo, Puebla 116
Huichols, the 66, **71**
    airstrips 75
    beads 82
    caves, god figures 73
    dress 72
    farm machinery 75
    music 75
    nearíkas 107, 108
    sites of worship 73
    symbols 73, 74

I

Iguala, Guerrero 126
incense 67, 70, 71
Independence Day 112, 126, 137
Independence of Mexico 13
Indian rites 66, 67, 69, 70, 71
Ixmiquílpan, Hidalgo 80
Ixtapalapa 118
ixtle 91

J

Jalisco 66, 71
Janitzio Island 132
    Day of the Dead ceremonies on 136-137
January events 113
Jiménez, Manuel 109
Juan Diego 138
Juarez, Benito 116, 127
Judas figures 100, 101, 108, 120-121
June events 125

K

kites 99

L

Labor Day 124
lacquer 93
ladinos 71, 76, 77
Last Supper, the 118
Las Tuxtlas 13
latex 85

lead 94
   soldiers 94
   miniatures 94
leather 94
Lent 115, 117
Lewis, Oscar 135
Lord of Sorrows, the 116
Lorenzo, Augustín 116

M

machete 109, 145
Magi, the 113
magicians 67, 69, 70
maguey 91, 98
March events 116
Marco Polo 141
market days, a listing 167-168
masks **95,** 112, 114, 115, 132
   of the State of Oaxaca 78
   Tiger 95
Mass of Glory 121, 123
matracas 120
Maundy Thursday 121
Mayas 85, 124
   Day of the Dead beliefs of 136
May events 124
Mayos 95
Mazatlán 115
medicine men 67
mestizos 71
Mexico City 14, 15, 35
Michoacán 36, 89, 104, 117, 126
miniatures 26
Ministry of Education 121
Mitla 114
mold-casting of clay 86
monigotes 138
Monte Alban, Oaxaca 88
Moors and Christians, Battle of 126
Morelos 117
moss, Spanish 104
moth balls, 110
mulito, Corpus Christi toy 90, 98, 125
Murillo, Gerardo 16, 17
music, Huichol 75
musicians 70

N

nacimiento 86, 92, 104, 107, 109, 115, 139, 144

Náhuatl 117
   language 66
National Academy of Arts 16
Nayarit 66, 71, 76
   San Juan Carapán 76
Nazareth 139
nearíkas 108
Nine Days of Christmas 143
Noche Buena 143
North American Indians 82
November events 128
nutshell miniatures 96

O

Oaxaca 14, 16, 57, 59, 77, 88, 89, 108, 126, 128, 139
   Regional Museum 78
Ocotlán, Oaxaca 87, 89
October events 127
ofrenda 128, 131, 132
ojo de dios 74
Olinalá, Guerrero 16, 82, 95
Orozco, José 135
Otomís 66-71

P

pagan beliefs 65
Pahuatlán, Hidalgo 71
palm leaves 70, 97
Palm Sunday 117, 118
Palm Sunday ornaments 98, 118
Pancho the Toymaker 15
panes de muertos 129, 131
Papantla, Vera Cruz 107, 125, 126
paper 98
   crêpe 99
   papel China 99
   papel de seda 99
   street banners 112
   tissue 69, 99
paper dolls 67, 69, 70, 71
papier mâché 14, 25, 91, 99, **100,** 101, 102, 108, 114, 121, 129, 132, 142
paraffin 108
Partir de la Vieja 123
Pastoral plays 143
Pátzcuaro, Michoacán 138
Paz, Octavio 12, 33, 65, 111, 127, 132, 135, 150
penitentes 118
Peru 74

petate mats 97, 103
piñatas 99, 103, 123, 141, 142
   Vasquez family, makers 143
pinwheels 146
pirotécnico 112, 145
Pomar, María Teresa 36
popular arts 17, 18, 36
Posada, José Guadalupe 135
posadas 139
   nineteenth century 140
pottery—see clay
pottery villages 88
prayer arrows 74
prayer discs 74
pre-Hispanic times 66
   customs 71
   incense burner 128
   pottery turtle-rattle 92
   sacred jaguar 82
Puebla 14, 108, 117
pulque, pulquerías 98

Q

quechquémetl 71

R

rabbit fur 102
rayado lacquer 93
reed 97, 103
Resurrection Day 120
rites, Indian 66, 67, 69, 70, 71
ritual objects 66
Rivera, Diego 17, 121, 132, 135
Rosca de Reyes 114
Rubin, Daniel de la Borbolla 14
rueda de fortuna 108
rush 97

S

Saint Anthony's Day 114
Saint John the Baptist 76, 126
San Bartólo Coyotepec, Oaxaca 82, 86, 89
San Cristóbal las Casas, Chiapas 66, 123
San José, Feast of 116
San Juan Carapán, Nayarit 76
San Marco Fair 123

San Miguel de Allende, Guanajuato 118, 131, 143
San Pablito, Puebla 66, 71
San Pablo, Oaxaca 114
Santa Clara del Cobre, Michoacán 89
Santa María Atzompa, Oaxaca 57, 59, 84, 89
Santa Prisca church, Taxco 118, 143
sapodilla tree 85
September events 127
Seris 66, 76
Seville, Spain 117
shamans 67, 69, 71, 72
shaping clay 86
Sierra Madre Occidental 66, 71, 82
Sierra Madre Oriental 66
Soldiers' Christ, the 116
Soledad church, Oaxaca 139
Sonora 76
sorcerers 69, 70, 71
Spain, New 13, 14
Spanish invasion 13, 71
Spanish missionaries 71
Spanish moss 104
Spirit of the Field ritual 70
Spirit of the House ritual 70
straw 104
surface texture, clay 87

T

Talpa de Allende, Jalisco 85
Tanajapa, Chiapas 76
tapa cloth 66
Tarahuama Indians 34
Tarascan Indians 89
Tarascan Day of the Dead ceremonies 136, 137
Taxco, Guerrero 116, 118
   posada 143
Tehuantepec, Oaxaca 114
tejamanil 108
tempera paints 105
Tenosique, Tabasco 85
Teotihuacán 115
Teotitlan del Valle, Oaxaca 114, 126
Tepaltzingo, Morelia 116
Tepeyac, Mexico 138
Three Kings, Day of 112-114, 144
tin 106
tissue paper 69, 99
Tlacotalpan, Vera Cruz 115
Tlacotepec, Puebla 126
Tlaquepaque, Jalisco 14
Toluca, Mexico 131

Tonalá, Chiapas 14
Toor, Frances 34, 72, 76
torito, little bull fireworks 148, 149
Totónac Indians 107
toy shop 26
toys, wheeled 13
    folk 25
    most antique 14
Tres Zapotes, Vera Cruz 13
tule 97
turtles (fireworks) 149
Tzintzuntzan, Michoacán 104, 115, 118

V

Valle de Mezquital 80
vanilla beans 107
Velasco family, tinsmiths 106
Vera Cruz 13, 115
Viceroys, Spanish 13
violin 75
Virgen de la Candelaría 115
Virgen de la Soledad 139
Virgen del Carmen 126
Virgin of Guadalupe 112, 138

W

wax, beeswax 82, 107
    paraffin 108
wire springs 108
Wise Men 144
witchcraft 65, 71
witch doctors 67
wood 108
    playthings 109, 110
worms in wood carvings 110

X

xalama tree 66

Y

Yaquis 95
Yucatán 85, 124, 136

Z

Zaachila, Oaxaca 116
Zacatecas 66, 71
Zapotecas 77, 78
    Day of the Dead beliefs 136
zempasúchitl, flower of the Dead 131
Zorilla, José 135